A POLITICAL EDUCATION

ALSO BY ANDRÉ SCHIFFRIN

L'edition sans editeurs Paris 1999
The Business of Books London/New York 2000
Le Controle de la parole Paris 2005

EDITED VOLUMES

The Fifties: Photos from Magnum
  (with Natalia Schiffrin) New York 1985
The Cold War and the Universities New York 1997
Conglomerates and the Media New York 1997
Correspondence—André Gide-Jacques Schiffrin, 1922-1950
  (with Alban Cerisier) Paris 2005

A
POLITICAL
EDUCATION

COMING OF AGE IN PARIS AND NEW YORK

ANDRÉ SCHIFFRIN

MELVILLE HOUSE PUBLISHING
HOBOKEN, NEW JERSEY

© ANDRÉ SCHIFFRIN, 2007

MELVILLE HOUSE PUBLISHING
300 OBSERVER HIGHWAY
THIRD FLOOR
HOBOKEN, NJ 07030

WWW.MHPBOOKS.COM

FIRST MELVILLE HOUSE PRINTING: MARCH 2007

BOOK DESIGN: BLAIR & HAYES

Library of Congress Cataloging-in-Publication Data

Schiffrin, André.
  A political education / André Schiffrin.
      p. cm.
  Includes bibliographical references.
  ISBN-13: 978-1-933633-15-2
  ISBN-10: 1-933633-15-8
  1. Schiffrin, André—Political and social views. 2. Schiffrin,
André—Childhood and youth.   3. Schiffrin, André—Homes
and haunts—France—Paris.   4. Publishers and publishing—
United States—Biography.   5. Paris (France)—Intellectual
life—20th century. 6. United States—Intellectual life—20th
century. I. Title.
  Z473.S36 2007
  070.5092—dc22
  [B]

                              2006101685

TO THE MEMORY OF MY PARENTS

ACKNOWLEDGMENTS

I am very grateful to my editors and publishers at Melville House, Dennis Johnson and Valerie Merians, for courageously taking on the task of publishing this footnote to our recent history. Their comments and suggestions have been a real help in the writing of this book.

I am also grateful to a number of readers who agreed to compare my account with their own memories of the period. These include some of my Friends Seminary schoolmates, such as Paul Chevigny and Antoinette King. Lore Segal has also been very helpful in discussing our common experience as refugees. Bob Rifkind looked at the memories of Yale that we share.

My colleagues Sara Bershtel, Joel Ariaratnam, and Andy Hsiao were kind enough to lay aside their heavy editorial load and to read early drafts, most helpfully. Finally, I had much help and encouragement from my family—my wife Maria Elena, who had to share the uncertainties and travails of writing this, and my daughters, Anya and Natalia, who were unfailingly enthusiastic from the start; my uncle, Serge Brodsky, read all this from a French perspective and caught what would have been many errors.

The thought of writing this book came to me after I had spent the year 2003 in Paris, a time that is described in this book's final chapter. I had already written a kind of professional auto-biography in 2000 called *The Business of Books*, about my role as a publisher and how that had changed along with the publishing business as a whole. But after my year in Paris I felt there was more to be said. I realized that I had resisted saying some things in my first book, partly because I hadn't wanted to write anything too close to my personal life, partly because I had kept from myself many aspects of my own turbulent history, and partly because I had reached that age at which people often find themselves looking back on their life and realizing how much of it had been left unexamined. Along with this was the deepening understanding that I knew far too little about my parents; that I had failed to ask them crucial questions when I was young and that now it was too late to do so.

This realization came slowly and in part indirectly. It started with my work in preparing a French edition of the decades-long correspondence between my father, Jacques Schiffrin, and his great friend André Gide. They had met in France in the 1920s—very early in my father's publishing career—and had worked together until my father's death in 1950. Gide is now considered by many to be the key author in prewar France, someone whose moral and intellectual challenges had been felt by a whole generation. I knew how much this friendship had meant to my father, but I had never seen all of their extensive correspondence. That is, while I had seen many of Gide's letters, which my father had meticulously kept, I had never read my father's answers. I had not been aware that they had been preserved in a Paris archive, in fact, until Alban Cerisier, the archivist for the great French publishing house Gallimard, where my father had worked, approached me about publishing the complete correspondence.

My father's numerous letters came as a shock to me. I had known that he had been very unhappy at leaving France in 1941, but he had kept from me just how miserable his existence in New York had been. I remembered him as a loving and encouraging father, someone absorbed in his work in spite of his serious illnesses. (He suffered from emphysema. In America, he was increasingly short of breath and exhausted as a result.) He had successfully kept from me his cares and his increasing sorrow at being unable to return to France. However, the very feelings he had kept from me, he had poured out in his letters to Gide. I was astonished not simply at the depth of his despair but at the fact that I had never suspected it. My childhood innocence had been infinitely greater than I could ever have thought possible.

And so I began to wonder: If I had been ignorant of such a crucial aspect of my youth, what else had I missed? As for myself, I knew that far from wanting to return to France, I had quickly come to feel totally Americanized. I thought that I had led the life of a typical young New Yorker. To be sure, my ideas and preferences were different from those of many of my friends, but that seemed perfectly normal to me. It didn't seem due to my having been born in France. My political, intellectual, and other attitudes seemed to fit into the America of the forties and fifties, even if only into its fringes. As I grew older, my attitude remained, to my mind, that of any committed citizen responding to the policies of the institutions in which we lived. I was sure that anyone else would have responded in the same way, had they only heard the arguments that had influenced me.

Likewise, I felt that in my close to fifty years in publishing, I had acted in the way that any devoted editor would have acted; that my battles and choices were typical responses to the changes that had been imposed on our profession, and that others in my position would have reacted the same way that I had. That none of this had been due to my French background.

It was the year I spent in Paris that made me question many of those assumptions. Though I still felt very much an American in Paris, I realized how much I also felt at home in France, particularly in its social and intellectual life. The French were quick to accept my dual nature and willing to listen to my views. As an outsider, I was able to say much—about France, about publishing and the media, about the U.S.—that they felt but often hesitated to express in public. I found myself playing an unexpected and, to me, welcome role in the debates about the changing nature of French media, and of the intellectual and political life there. But I also realized that while I was indeed an outsider, I nonetheless shared many of the underlying French assumptions. For example, I had the same feelings about the role of the state, and about the degree to which France should resist or even reject some of the outside forces that were gradually changing much of its daily life.

From that side of the ocean I also felt a deepening awareness of how impermeable America had become to outside influence. In a course I taught on how to read a newspaper at L'Institut d'études politique in Paris—better known as Sciences Po—I could see each day how American papers not only rejected European opinion, but felt it was their duty to lecture and castigate the Continent for its anticapitalist values, for its shocking adherence to independence from American influence and to the welfare state, even for its acceptance of leisure and nonwork time as an essential part of life.

Thus, while still feeling that any reasonable person should have shared my reactions, I began to wonder how French I really was; how many of the country's values I had internalized, how much of my life had actually been that of an outsider coping with American assumptions. Going back to my childhood and adolescence, I saw a set of experiences and thoughts that I had never closely examined; a pattern began to emerge that gave me a different slant on the life I had led.

That life had been devoted primarily to politics and to ideas. Not electoral politics—I had never thought of running for anything, nor even of joining anyone's campaign, as my children had done. But it was a life that nonetheless had centered on what was happening in American politics and in the politics of the rest of the world. So this book is an attempt to reexamine my life, primarily my formative years during the crucial postwar period from 1948 to 1968—which, coincidentally, was in many ways the formative period of the modern political debate. There had been numerous accounts of the subsequent period—the Vietnam era and its aftermath—but far fewer of the earlier one. At the same time, I did not want to attempt a political history of the second half of the century. That has been done extremely well by many historians, a number of whom I have published. And in spite of my years studying to be an historian, I felt I had nothing new to contribute in the way of analytic historical scholarship. (I am enough of an editor to know when to reject a manuscript, even if it's mine.) Simply, I felt I had personal experience that shed light on some of our common experiences. This book, then, is primarily a political memoir.

Here I have deliberately left out some major elements of my personal life, close to fifty years of marriage to a marvelous wife and the lives of our two daughters, of whom we're very proud. Those stories belong elsewhere.

Family albums are treacherous things. They lie there quietly, over the years, waiting to be shown to bored grandchildren and other relatives. But like Poe's purloined letter, they contain unexpected truths, unbeknownst to the innocent owner, that can be discerned by the knowledgeable detective.

For years I had worked with a young American photo-historian named Michael Lesy, who became well-known in the early 1970s when I published his PhD thesis as a book we called *Wisconsin Death Trip*. Lesy had found a stash of glass plates taken by a small-town photographer at the end of the nineteenth century and had fashioned a brilliant psycho-history of the period from this forgotten trove. The book became a bestseller and established Lesy's reputation, but he found it a hard act to follow. When he decided that family albums might contain the same kind of neglected material, I mentioned that I had one. Lesy was interested.

He sat next to me on our living-room couch and closely examined the bedraggled red cover, stained with cigarette burns, over some of which my mother had pasted photos of Charlie Chaplin as Hitler (in *The Great Dictator*). The album, which I'd looked at unthinkingly dozens of times, was divided into two sections. The first, which covered my first six years, were all set in France and seemed to depict an incredibly idyllic time: Our large sunny Paris apartment with my toy-filled room; holiday photos in Belgium with Aldous Huxley and his family; a day at the beach in Royan with my mother Simone and her friends next to me as an infant. That last was a glamorous series of images that my mother loved, and that I remember being told had been taken by a fashion photographer. They looked it.[1]

In short, the first section of the album showed the carefree life that I dimly remembered—the reflections of a happy, comfortable, and well-off childhood, a classic Parisian boyhood. Frequent trips to the Normandy beaches, merry-go-rounds in the Tuileries, the little sailboat basin in the Luxembourg Gardens....

It was a time that must have appeared in retrospect no less idyllic to my parents: My father, recently freed of the financial worries of running his own publishing company and instead now

---

[1] But I knew nothing more about that series of photos until late 2005, when I heard from a curator in Hamburg who was preparing an exhibit of the work of Alfred Otto Wolfgang Schulze, a German photographer and painter who went by the name of Wols after taking refuge in France in the thirties. Thus, I discovered that it was Wols who had taken the portraits of my mother and me that we had cherished, and that they had been published in a French magazine. My mother was extraordinarily striking at the time. Malraux had called her the most beautiful woman in Paris. (Family friends teased me about this—when I was three I had a very pretty young nanny, called Aurora. Who was more beautiful, I was asked, Aurora or Simone? Learning diplomacy at an early age, I answered that Simone was more beautiful but Aurora was newer.) The catalogue of Wols' photos included a series of very romantic portraits of French women he had taken in 1936 and 1937. Next to my mother's photo is one of a French actress named Sonia Mosse. The accompanying text outlines her career, then states that she was deported to the Lublin-Majdanek extermination camp, where she was killed on March 30, 1943.

working at Gallimard, the biggest publisher in France, directing the prestigious classic series he'd begun, called the Pléiade, for what he assumed would be the rest of his life; my mother occupied with her only son and her extended family. I can think of no unhappy event they ever mentioned about those prewar years. The album seemed an accurate reflection of all our lives.

The next section of the album consisted of photographs taken in New York City in the fall of 1941. The first few show the small apartment on Riverside Drive where we lived upon our arrival. The rest were taken in the surprisingly inexpensive and rent-controlled flat that my parents subsequently found on the corner of Park Avenue and Seventy-fifth Street. It was one of the few low-rise, tenement-like apartments that could be found on the Avenue, and it still is. Whenever I pass the building now, its fire escape stands out as an anachronistic reminder to me of another era.

As I looked back over the photos with Michael Lesy, I realized how bare both of these places looked, except for my mother's large jewelry worktable, at which she worked day and night. This was the background for my own first American portraits, playing in a military uniform or with my toy soldiers. Clearly I had decided that I would no longer face an enemy unarmed. But the very familiarity of the pictures had kept me from noticing how poor and sad the apartments looked, how very different from the images of our prewar life in Paris. Lesy seemed fascinated by it all, though I was happy when he later decided not to include any of the photos in his book. (I was relieved lest our destitution become part of the public domain, making us successors to the photos of dead babies that had made his first book so notorious.)

* * *

What strikes me in retrospect is how unaware of the album's message I had been, how little I had noted the contrast in our lives, how oblivious I had been to the spare décor of our New York existence. In looking through these pages hundreds of times, neither I nor my parents nor my children nor other family and friends had ever commented on any of this.

Something else about the album that now seems obvious struck me as well: It contained very few photographs of my parents' lives before their marriage. They had both apparently left behind their previous lives when they came together. My father, Jacques, had been born in Russia in 1892, beside the Caspian Sea in Baku, the oil-rich capital of Azerbaijan. His father had gone there to work as a longshoreman. Eventually, my grandfather had been struck by the fact that the Caspian surrounding the city was always aflame. Surely something could be done with the oil waste that was being dumped daily into the water? He met a young Swedish chemist, Alfred Nobel, who had been lured to Baku by the oil rush, and set about learning from him the basics of chemistry. He found that the waste could be turned into usable petrochemicals, so my grandfather began approaching the oil producers with offers to buy it. They were amazed at his stupidity but agreed readily. Thus guaranteed a steady supply of inexpensive raw materials, the Schiffrin petrochemical works was soon flourishing, supplying tar and other products to much of Russia. My uncle Simon Schiffrin reported going back to the Soviet Union in the 1950s and finding barrels in the Leningrad harbor that still bore the family name.

In sum, my father grew up in very comfortable surroundings. The few family photos we have of that time show a prosperous group leading the life of the very rich. Each summer they would take the train to Switzerland for their vacation. Their servants filled their train compartments with the pillows and linen that were required for the three-day journey. On shorter holidays, they would repair to the family dacha, or country house, in Russian Finland.

In 2003, my older daughter, Anya, who is fascinated by her roots, persuaded me to return to Baku. We found the former Nobel and Rockefeller mansions, which date back to the oil rush at the end of the nineteenth century. We also discovered the old Schiffrin family house in the center of town. It surrounded a spacious courtyard, and one could still see the large, sun-filled rooms that had once included a ballroom and other grand gathering spaces. The beautiful building Anya and I found ourselves examining was now a very busy and welcoming abortion clinic.

The family later moved to St. Petersburg and, as the First World War approached, my father decided to go to Geneva to study law and, I assume, to escape the Czarist draft. Those Swiss years seem to have been very happy ones. He had more than enough money to live very comfortably and made many close friends, among them the Swiss psychologist Jean Piaget, as well as, I gather, a great many women. He cut a dashing figure, was a skilled skater, and led what seems to have been a carefree student's life. I know little more about this period, however, and am puzzled by some of its mementos. For example, a Bible presented to my father by Rabindranath Tagore, the Indian philosopher; it has a long, very high-minded dedication by Tagore dated 1918.

They must have been good friends, but I don't know how this came about.

Things changed for my father when the war ended. Russia's revolutionary government nationalized the family holdings, leaving him nearly penniless in Europe. Ironically, the only money the family still had came from their shares of Nobel's dynamite works, which they had obtained in an exchange for shares from the now-nationalized Schiffrin oil company. (Poor Nobel got the worse of the bargain, but he seems to have survived nonetheless.) My father went from Geneva to Monte Carlo and decided to try his luck at the casino. Acting like a character out of Dostoevsky (whom he would later translate), he left a large part of his limited funds on a single number on the roulette board and, amazingly, won. Rather than go home happily, he decided to leave the money on the same number one more time—a reckless move that I would never have been capable of. But against all odds the number came up again, and my father found himself with enough money to last for a couple of years.

He decided to move from Geneva to Florence and somehow got a job there as the secretary to Bernard Berenson. They worked together for several years, and as a result of this collaboration my father would later publish Berenson's *Italian Portraits of the Renaissance*. While in Florence he also was hired by Peggy Guggenheim to teach her Russian. However, when it became clear that he would do no more than that, Guggenheim fired him. (Her memoirs describe this without rancor, though later they reveal a less attractive aspect of her personality when she describes her wartime glee at being able to buy so many paintings cheaply from Jewish artists desperate to flee Hitler's Europe.)

Having rejected Guggenheim's advances, my father fell in love with, and married, a Russian pianist, Yura Guller, whom he had met while playing the cello in chamber-music groups. Guller had won the first prize of the Conservatoire de Paris in 1909 and had a promising future ahead of her. During their early years together, she enchanted my father's friend André Gide with her mastery of Chopin and taught him how to play and understand Chopin's compositions, for which Gide was endlessly grateful, according to his biographers.

My father was also accomplished enough to be considering a career as a cellist, but Guller was understandably obsessed with her own possibilities, and one such professional turned out to be more than enough in a marriage: They agreed to divorce after a few years. By the oddest of coincidences, I was to meet her once, many, many years later. My family and I were spending the summer in Dartington in Southern England, where my wife had grown up. Dartington was famous for its summer music school, and there on its program of visiting artists was Guller's name. I went to see her after her performance and introduced myself. I think she was amused to meet me but far from deeply moved; our links were too distant and tenuous. All I now have of her is a compact disc of her Chopin recordings, its cover photo showing a striking, dark-haired woman.

From Italy, my father moved to Paris in the early twenties, where he decided to try his hand at publishing. He began by serving a kind of apprenticeship with the art publisher Henri Piazza. After a short time, however, he felt ready to strike out on his own and in 1922 formed a new publishing house, which he called Éditions de la Pléiade. The name came not from mythology or

French literary history, as has often been assumed, but from a group of classic Russian poets. With no authors at his disposal, he began with a series of Russian titles translated into French by himself and friends. It was at the very beginning of the Éditions de la Pléiade that my father got in touch with André Gide, whose help he sought in translating what would be his first book, Pushkin's *The Queen of Spades*. The books were lavishly illustrated, some by Russian artists living in Paris, and they had stunning typography, which my father himself designed. (In the fifties, I happened to visit the Soviet Pavilion at the Venice Biennale and saw an exhibit of these books—surprisingly, displayed as examples of Russian art in the postwar period.[2])

After the success of his early, deluxe editions, my father had the idea of publishing a series of books, leather-bound and on Bible paper, consisting primarily of French classics. The series became known as the Bibliotheque de la Pléiade, and it remains to this day one of the mainstays of French publishing. The idea was to collect in each volume the basic works of one great author in a carefully established and annotated text, yet at the same time the books were to be relatively inexpensive—to buy the Pléiade Proust would be less expensive than to buy all the volumes in the regular editions, for example—and more portable. Gide often spoke of carrying them around in his pocket. Beginning with a volume of Baudelaire, my father gradually went on to publish all

---

[2] As a sideline, my father also started a small art gallery, the Galerie de la Pléiade, where he featured the work of these artists. Later he expanded the role of the gallery to include the work of others, giving the artist Wols his first solo show. The gallery soon became one of Paris' leading art venues, particularly for photography, at the height of the Surrealist era.

of the major works of French literature. He then expanded the series to include translated works; at present the Pléiade includes nearly all of the world's classic literature (though the new editions are far more scholarly and much more expensive than my father had originally intended).

The Pléiade was an instant and enormous success, such a success that Jacques soon ran through the small capital he'd raised from investors (primarily family and friends) and didn't have the up-front funds necessary to print sufficient quantities of books fast enough. He was still on good terms with Peggy Guggenheim, and she invested as well. To pay her back in part, he gave her six hundred copies of *The Queen of Spades*—which she tried unsuccessfully to sell to Parisian bookstores. Happily, the book later became a great success, and Jacques bought back and resold her copies.

But in spite of such maneuvers, my father ultimately had to look for more financing, and he approached several of Paris' larger, more established publishing houses. In 1933, my father joined Gallimard, perhaps the most prestigious firm in Paris, through the intervention of Gide, who had been closely involved with the firm since its origins. He stayed there until the German occupation in 1940, when the German "ambassador," Otto Abetz, issued orders for the takeover of key French institutions, Gallimard among them. The firm was to be "Aryanized." On August 20, 1940, barely two months into the German occupation of Paris, my father was dismissed in a two-line letter from the owner, Gaston Gallimard. Jacques was one of the two Jews in the firm and their departure led to the increasing role of French fascists in running Gallimard. It also led to the changes chronicled in our family album.

* * *

My mother's life had been much less eventful. Her father, Oscar Heymann, had come to Paris from Strasbourg in Alsace-Lorraine as a penniless pedlar, ordered by his father to some-how earn enough money for his sister's dowries. Gradually, he built a successful business dealing in lace and trimmings, which allowed him to raise my mother, who was born in 1906, and her two sisters and younger brother in the comfortable suburb of Neuilly in a vast, luxurious apartment that included a billiards room, proof of their bourgeois achievements. Like most French girls of the post-First World War period, my mother never went to college, though she certainly partook of the intellectual fer-vor of the period; one of my favorite of her stories was of lining up at the local bookstore as each new volume of Proust's *Remembrance of Things Past* appeared.

But my maternal grandfather was a very strict father of the old school. If he ever caught my mother leaving the house wearing even a soupçon of makeup, he would wet his handkerchief and erase all the offending traces. My mother, however, was deter-mined to break away and, hearing from friends that there was an opening for a secretary in a new publishing house, she climbed the stairs to the sixth-floor, one-room office housing the fledgling Editions de la Pléiade and applied for the job. She would later remember that each landing on the long staircase had a sign say-ing that thé offices were just above. My father was immediately struck by her beauty and, recently divorced from his first wife, Yura, he promptly offered her the job, even though she confessed that she had no previous work experience and didn't even know how to type. My parents were married soon thereafter, in 1929, and they embarked on what was by all accounts a joyful first few years.

As it did for millions of others, the war would drastically alter their circumstances, turning their world upside down. In 1939, my father was drafted into the French army, in spite of being nearly fifty years old and suffering from emphysema. His fragile health was not improved by having to live in spartan barracks outside of Paris. Yet all this seems to have barely impinged on my life. My parents managed to conceal a great deal of what was happening from me, and to turn much of what they couldn't conceal into a child's game. To distract me from his departure and the disruption of our lives, my father made me a child's version of his uniform, although adding numerous medals. It was something I boasted of in my letters to Gide (who by then had become one of my father's closest friends). Later, when my father was back in Paris during the first German air raids, he deputized me as an "assistant air-raid warden," and thus my memories of those bombardments are of scurrying down to our cellar as if in a thrilling adventure, rather than in actual danger. My parents even arranged for me to celebrate my fifth birthday a day early, on June 13, 1940—the day before the German army entered Paris.

It puzzles me to this day how they managed to so fully conceal from me their fears and anxieties. And I doubt that I am denying what I experienced, as my father's letters regularly refer to me playing happily in the background throughout those difficult years, including during what must have been my parents' most harrowing experience: fleeing the Nazis.

My father had no doubts as to what would happen if we stayed in France. He knew about the concentration camps and must have heard of the systematic murder that was already taking place in the East of Europe. Some million-and-a-half Jews had been killed on the spot by the German army before the extermination camps had been built. He was also acutely aware of the growing French anti-Semitism and xenophobia, fanned first by the right-wing press and later by the Vichy government itself. My family were typical secularized Jews, opposed to all religions, following none of the rites or customs of Judaism. In Russia, many Jewish intellectuals had considered rabbis to be conveyors of superstition and irrationality. Both of my parents were aware of their origins, of course, but they were among the many in Europe who became Jews because of Hitler.

Shortly after the Germans marched into Paris on my birthday, they took over our apartment and we had to leave Paris. To me, our encounters with the German soldiers, even in Normandy, where we first took refuge, were pleasant enough. I remember the friendly young soldiers who, in those early months, were under strict orders to ingratiate themselves with the local population. Being polite, even flirtatious, to my mother did not require much effort. It was all smiles and blandishments at the outset.

I don't really remember being worried until we prepared to cross from the German occupied zone of the north to the erroneously-termed Free Zone, theoretically under the control of the collaborationist Vichy government. We had fake papers, and I had to memorize a new name. I remember sitting in the dark stalls of the bathroom in the border post, where I endlessly repeated it to myself, but in the end it was never asked of me.

Once in the Midi, we stayed in St. Tropez in an apartment that my parents had rented for winter vacations in the tower of the Chateau Suffren. My mother and father continued to try to distract me. On one occasion this led to the only other moment of real anxiety that I can remember clearly: when they took me to see the new Disney movie, *Dumbo*. American films were apparently still available in Vichy France. But like many Disney films, it emphasized children being separated from their parents, and it left me terrified for days. My mother and father, meanwhile, were luckier with their exposure to American popular culture. The novel *Gone with the Wind* had just appeared in a French translation, and it proved to be the best possible escape reading, in both senses of the word. When my father had finished a page, he would tear it out and hand it on to my mother.

We remained in St. Tropez while waiting for our visas to come through. The tiny village was beautiful and still unspoiled then, devoid of the ostentatious display of the post-Bardot years. Now, the harbor lacks sufficient room for all the yachts seeking port. And though this was a time of endless strain and duress for my parents, I have only pleasant memories. I remember the excitement of seeing the horses of the French cavalry, which were installed in the stables of the Chateau. The Chateau is still there. I have visited it several times over the decades. Once I even went back to our old apartment, and I saw again the clear view of the unending Mediterranean that we had from our windows. And although we were hungry during the winter of 1940, I remember the idyllic walks down mimosa-lined country paths where, with the help of a local lad, I learned to scramble up the pine trees to get the cones that contained precious, edible nuts. The images of those exquisitely scented forests stay with me, too—the perfume of the mimosa mingling with the hot, rich odors of the pine-needle-covered ground.

For my parents, of course, it was all very trying. From St. Tropez my father traveled to and from Marseilles, hoping to somehow book passage on a ship to America. But we were to find ourselves trapped for months, anxiously waiting. It was a time of heartbreaking false starts, waiting for exit visas and tickets, each threatening to expire before the others were obtained.

As my father wrote to Gide—referring to me by his nickname for me, Minouche—on May 11, 1941:

> *Five days ago we received, in St. Tropez, a telegram saying we could leave for the United States on a ship from Marseille May 15. Therefore we needed to leave for Marseille immediately. We spent the night packing our cases . . . and left at five in the morning. Since arriving in Marseille, we have undergone a new kind of torture. Arrangements are made and then unmade in the same day. That is, once we have gotten all the necessary papers, visas, ticket, passports, etc., the next step fails and all is lost. To save what seems lost forever, I drag myself through the streets in the hope that I will meet someone who knows someone. Once or twice I've had luck and a friend I hadn't seen for twenty years turns out to know someone, on some committee or in a consulate. And there we are, at nine this morning all seemed lost and at eleven another phone call came saying we might have a solution the next day. Thus until the very last minute we will not know whether we have everything that we need in order to leave. It's all terrible. And Minouche insists on playing during all of this.*

In her memoirs, Peggy Guggenheim writes of meeting my father at about this time, presumably in Marseilles. Safe herself, thanks to her American passport (the U.S. had not yet entered the war), she notes that she had never met anyone so depressed and worried.

From the start, in fact, my father's good friends were as helpful as they could be, but they did not all realize the danger that staying in France would have entailed. Gide commented to friends that he hoped that Jacques would not regret having left, and Roger Martin du Gard sent numerous friendly and encouraging letters urging him not to worry; that staying in France would not be as bad as all that. (Though later, in November, 1941, Martin du Gard wrote of the hardship of living in France, saying that "not only are we going to starve, but we will freeze as well.") But neither man had any understanding of the dangers that Jews, particularly those of foreign origin, were facing by staying in France. Mass deportations of 75,000 people, including some 1,200 schoolchildren, to the extermination camps from which only a small number would return would start in July, 1942.

What also surprised me on reading the complete file of my father's letters to Gide was seeing how, during all of these years of terrible stress, my father continued to write to Gide about the most minor of publishing details. Gide's journals had just appeared in the Pléiade, the first time a living author had been so honored, and they had been a huge success. Gide constantly found typos and words that he wanted changed in the next printing. Letters were exchanged, first to and from my father's army barracks and then later to and from the many towns to which we moved after leaving Paris. Gide seemed oblivious of the disruption that had been brought to our lives. When my father was living in the army barracks, Gide would write several times asking that copies of his books be sent to various friends and acquaintances throughout the world, as if my father was still in his comfortable and well-staffed offices at Gallimard.

And it wasn't just his close friends Gide and Martin du Gard with whom he kept up a steady correspondence. By an odd coincidence, I was approached recently by the biographer Louise Borden, who was writing a book about Hans and Margret Rey, the authors of the very popular *Curious George* children's books. She had found, in the library of the University of Southern Mississippi, of all places, a file of my father's correspondence with the Reys. (He had been their editor. In addition to his work on the Pléiade, my father had launched Gallimard's children's list in 1933. Following the work he had done in the twenties, he found Russian classics for children, and published stories by Chekhov and Tolstoy. But he soon expanded to French authors and began the very popular series of books by Marcel Ayme as well as books by Henri Bosco. He also launched a children's almanac, the *Albums du gai savoir.*) The Reys' books would eventually be among the most popular, and my father had published the first of them. Indeed, I had been the very first reader and had urged my father to go ahead. The books had subsequently sold 30 million copies in the U.S., so my first try at publishing proved far more successful than would any of my adult efforts. The Reys were also trying to flee from France, yet the letters continued to flow, from ever-changing addresses. At a time when the British were evacuating Dunkirk, letters to the British publishing house Chatto and Windus were still being exchanged. I suppose dealing with these day-to-day publishing issues, long after he had been fired from

Gallimard, allowed my father to maintain some feeling of stability, but it still astonishes me to see how he found time for these endless details.

Luckily for us, we were put in touch with the heroic American Varian Fry, probably through Gide. Fry, a journalist, had been sent to Marseilles in August, 1940, on behalf of the Emergency Rescue Committee, a group organized in New York by Reinhold Neibuhr, Thomas Mann's daughter Erika Mann, and others. The group in New York raised money (including, interestingly enough, a healthy donation from the Book of the Month Club) that Fry then used to help as many people as possible—Jews, artists, and writers, as well as the German social-democrat and union leaders who were at great risk because of France's shameful agreement in the armistice treaty to "surrender on demand" anyone requested by the Germans—to escape the Nazis by boat to either Lisbon or Casablanca, where they could book passage to America.

Fry's sponsors wanted him to bring over as many famous names as possible. Among the first he approached, Picasso and Matisse had no interest in leaving (and lived through the occupation, as it turned out, perfectly safely). Even Marc Chagall, who as a foreign-born Jew was clearly in danger, hesitated a very long time before agreeing to go (which he did only after he was arrested by French police and then released before being handed over to the Gestapo, thanks to Fry's intervention.)

But Fry, much to his credit, wanted to save as many *people* as possible, not just the most famous. My father made it onto Fry's list, I suspect, through the intercession of Gide and his friend the renegade ex-Communist Boris Souvarine, who was a trusted guarantor of political correctness, since Fry was determined not to help Communists. (Communists, he assumed, could flee to Russia—where, it turned out, many would be at risk as well. And the State Department, reluctant to admit any refugees in the first place, would certainly have vetoed their applications.)

In any case, though we never had the chance to meet Fry, we made it onto his list of the two thousand or so people he was able to rescue, along with Souvarine himself, Chagall, Hannah Arendt, Max Ernst, Marcel Duchamp, André Breton, Wanda Landowska, the family of Thomas Mann, and many others. It was his help that cut through the Gordian knot of visa applications and ticket purchases, which seemed increasingly unbreakable, and after months of waiting we found ourselves leaving Marseilles on a boat bound for America.

The departure from France could not have been more humiliating, though everyone was vastly relieved to be on their way at last. Though my mother did not mention it until much later, she was greatly shaken by the shouts of "dirty kikes" that were hurled at us by the longshoremen as our ship left Marseilles. Such a betrayal by our countrymen seemed unthinkable and deeply hurtful. The shouts must have been as painful to the German refugees, who were the majority of our fellow passengers. I remember seeing the trays of swastika-stamped passports waiting to be inspected.

The ship that was to take us to the United States from Marseilles, however, stopped in Casablanca and did not continue on its planned transatlantic crossing. We were once again stranded, and this time it looked as if there would be no escape, since the Vichy government still controlled Casablanca (as everyone who has seen the film *Casablanca* knows). Claiming a dearth of hotel rooms in the city, the Vichy government forced all emigrants to Morocco to stay in internment camps in the desert. Once again, my father had to scramble for tickets on another ship even as our money ran out, and once again he had to enlist the help of every connection he could. And once again it was Gide who came through, not only with financial assistance but with the offer of a friend's apartment in the city. It allowed us to spend the time—which stretched into months—in relative comfort, albeit in dreadful anxiety, and finally my father was able to obtain passage for us on a ship that took us first to Lisbon and then, finally, to America.

As far as I was concerned, my only setback during the endless crossing to America was dropping my Donald Duck doll into a puddle of vomit; it became irremediably nauseating and had to be cast overboard. Meanwhile, I was unaware of the horrendous conditions into which my father and the other men were crammed. The ship's owners, having charged vast amounts for a ticket, had crowded as many people as they could into a stifling, airless hold where they were stacked on bunks frighteningly reminiscent of those in photographs that later came out of the concentration camps. There were constant fights in this squalid atmosphere as people sought space in which to breathe and live from day to day. In reading Victor Brombert's memoirs, *Trains of Thought,* I saw how commonplace this experience had been. His description of his crossing could have been mine (though he notes that the most aggressive and difficult passengers were those who had been interned in German concentration camps and were determined to protect themselves against their fellow passengers). Basically, each crossing had the same story. The refugees were deprived even of the originality of their suffering. Everyone had the same experience and, as a result, no one spoke about it once in America. After all, we were lucky to have escaped.

Hannah Arendt, in her marvelous and inexplicably unavailable essay on refugee rage in *The Jew as Pariah*, was one of the few to speak about this phenomenon. She was perhaps the first to note the irony of the silence that the refugees imposed on themselves, just as the first prisoners to be released from Dachau before the war dared not describe what had happened to them— although, of course, they had been threatened by the Nazis into their silence by warning that describing their ordeal would lead to their being arrested again. (It is striking to see in the Hollywood films of the period, made, after all, primarily by Jews, that the refugees are nearly always figures of fun, with their thick foreign accents and lack of familiarity with American ways. Even *Casablanca*, one of the most committed of American films, includes a scene in which an aged German couple assiduously practice their hopelessly fractured English under Walter Slezak's benevolent eye.)

* * *

When we finally arrived in New York on August 20, 1941, my mother's beauty was able to cut through the general apathy about refugees: A photographer from one of New York's afternoon newspapers spotted us, and our photo appeared in the next day's *World Telegram*. By then I was suitably thin, and my spindly legs made a pathetic contrast to my mother's Parisian chic. REFUGEES HERE TELL is all I have left of the headline, which must have been among the last of its kind to appear: Within three months of our arrival, Pearl Harbor would put an end to the trickle of exiles who would be allowed in.

For us, however, once we docked in New York, things immediately seemed more secure. On leaving the ship I was given a bottle of amazingly rich American milk, my first taste of the land of plenty. My father's brother Simon and his sister Lyolene had both preceded us to New York. Our first nights were spent in the Adams Hotel on East Eighty-sixth Street, in the home of Lyolene, a once-famous fashion designer. (She had established a well-regarded firm on the Place Vendôme and had been lured to America before the war to work for a major American designer.) Perhaps because they felt so much safer, my parents decided that I could spend the first evening alone in our room, while they went down to join the family—a mad decision, even though they had always joked about my self-assuredness. I asked how I could rejoin them, if need be. They told me that I had only to tell the elevator man, "Three, please." Though this seemed simple enough, I had no inkling of how English should be spoken and tried to think of a version that I could muster. I decided to myself that if I said the French words for cherry and plug, *cerise* and *prise*, and said them quickly enough, I might get away with it. Needless to say, within a few minutes of my parents' departure, I had had enough of solitude and tried my first words of English on the befuddled elevator man. Either he understood, or—more likely, I now realize—he remembered the floor on which my parents had gotten off. My first evening in my new homeland had ended in success, but it had not been without its unexpected hazards.

Upon our arrival, my parents had been warmly welcomed by other French writers such as the Catholic philosopher Jacques Maritain (whom my father would later publish at Pantheon Books) and others who were happy to see one of the prominent publishers from their world in their new community. But without the funds to set up on his own immediately, my father initially found work with firms that were publishing books in French in New York, such as Brentano's. In time, he would start publishing a few books in French under his own name, something that brought great relief to many in the exile community. The musician and composer Nadia Boulanger and others would write to him of their pleasure at seeing these books.

But all that would bring in only a very little money, and it became necessary for my mother to work, too. Though she had never really worked in Paris, except for that brief spell as my father's secretary, she had untried skills. She had always had an exceptional sense of style, more daring than most but still the embodiment of Parisian chic. So, soon after we settled in New York, she started out knitting fashionable garments for clients she found through friends. Then she discovered that in the new wartime economy, shortages would appear in unlikely places. Her friends in the fashion world told her that metal for buttons was no longer available, so Simone found that she could mold beautiful brooches and buttons from, appropriately enough, plaster of Paris. She copied classic French jewels and invented new patterns that she would then paint. These worked remarkably well, and soon our living room was a busy workshop in which a number of friends and acquaintances helped her. My mother needed every available hour to fill the ever-larger orders for her creations, and the apartment was crowded and hectic, with people working day and night.

My parents soon decided that this was no place for a child and, learning of a small boarding house for French refugee children in Montclair, New Jersey, they decided to send me there. I was appalled by this prospect of separation and argued strongly against it, saying that I could be a happy latchkey child and wait if need be on the doorstep. The last thing I wanted to do was move again; fear of being uprooted was the one trauma that I clearly felt (when some friends of my parents asked if I wanted a bicycle, I told them it would have to be a foldable one so that I could take it with me when next we had to move). But in an incredible show of obtuseness, my parents insisted that New York was hopeless and that being with French children my age would be infinitely better. I suppose the press of work and the uncertainty of our situation made them hope to shelter me in some calmer atmosphere, but as far as I was concerned, it was the worst of all possible outcomes.

Montclair in those days was a classic American white suburb. With the other boys from our boarding house, I would report each morning to my public school, where, in just a few months of what is now called "immersion studies," I learned to speak English. It was easy for me to concentrate purely on that, since my few months in a French kindergarten had put me ahead of my classmates in math and reading. Perhaps in part because of my anger at being torn from my parents, I was not at all ready to Americanize myself. I kept my fingers firmly crossed when made to recite the Pledge of Allegiance, and I felt a kind of schadenfreude when we all were taught to kneel under our desks during an air-raid drill. At last, I felt, the Americans will learn what war is like. I kept to myself my proud background as an assistant air-raid warden in Paris.

Not that there weren't closer brushes with the reality of war. During my occasional weekends with my parents, they would take me on explorations of the beaches of Long Island. They had been delighted to learn about Fire Island, whose vast, wild beaches were still relatively unknown to tourists and completely deserted out of season. They were as lovely as anything we had seen in Normandy, and they were closer to our home. My parents found an inexpensive boarding house where we could go with friends, and, late one afternoon, we were happily strolling down the beach when we were suddenly hailed by a very nervous young sentry. "You're lucky I didn't shoot you!" he said by way of greeting. Thus did we learn that a German submarine had recently landed nearby and unloaded a cargo of spies and saboteurs (all of whom were later captured and executed), and that the beach had been declared off-limits after dusk. The sentry seemed especially alarmed to encounter a group of people chatting in a foreign language, French or German being the same to him, although my presence must have seemed out of place—saboteurs were unlikely to bring a child, or even a midget. In any event, after a stern warning, he let us go, leaving us surprised by our one encounter with America in arms.

My parents were also puzzled by their discovery, at the end of another beach, that a barbed-wire fence prevented our walking any farther. But this was not a military obstacle. Beyond the boundaries of Ocean Beach lay what we were told was a "restricted community." Unable to understand this warning, my parents asked the locals and discovered that our neighboring hamlet was forbidden to Jews. After the openness of New York City, this show of nativist anti-Semitism was a shock, though not one they ever discussed with me. I wonder how they reacted to the irony that, after having had such difficulty in reaching America, they would find parts of it still forbidden to them.

During those first years in America, first in Montclair and then at home in Manhattan, I still felt a strong loyalty to France. My uncle Simon Schiffrin, a noted film producer best known for the French thirties classic *Le Quai des Brumes,* had gone to work for the Office of Strategic Services (OSS) film unit and then the Free French propaganda office in London. There, he had gotten me a signed photo of Charles de Gaulle that I kept in a place of honor in my room. I also carved the cross of Lorraine into my chest of drawers and kept a French flag in my room. I was eager to help the war effort in whatever way I could, and I saved my pennies to take to the French relief agency that was housed in the Villard mansion behind St. Patrick's Cathedral. In those days, the Catholic Church had not yet colonized the buildings, and a large cross of Lorraine stood above the main entrance where the Cardinal's cross would hang in later years (and where, later still, Bennett Cerf would install Random House). France Forever and the other pro-de Gaulle groups were all at work in the building where I myself would later work. During the years in which America recognized the Vichy government, which was to end with the American invasion of French North Africa in 1942, supplies of vitamins were allowed through to French schoolchildren, and I felt a strong need to get as much money as I could from our friends to help in that effort.

Years later, I was to learn from Eleanor Clark, an author I published, that behind the charitable operations, the Villard mansion served as a front for the OSS—the honorable predecessor to the CIA—in its efforts to direct espionage and sabotage behind enemy lines in France. Eleanor, who was the wife of Robert Penn Warren, had had a checkered career, having spent some time in Mexico City as Trotsky's secretary. But in those heady days, that was not held against her and may indeed have been a plus. True to the obligations of her secret work, she never told me exactly what they were up to in those luxurious offices. But even in retrospect, it's encouraging to think that more was being planned for France than the shipment of vitamins.

Beyond my visits to the Free French headquarters, there was a limit to what an eight-year-old could do for the war effort. Each week, like millions of other children, I would stick a saving stamp in my album, and the $25 savings bond was invariably the ideal present from adults. When a call went out to donate old car tires, I dutifully stripped the minuscule rubber tires from my toy cars. (I still find it hard to throw away a rubber band.) Years later I felt personally betrayed when I read that similar drives in England, for scrap metal and the like, had been devised by Lord Beaverbrook as simply a way to mobilize public opinion; to make everyone feel a part of the war effort. It made me wonder whether, in America, the metal foil from my father's cigarette packets that I so carefully rolled into snowball-like collections was ever used.

Needless to say, I was not the only one in the family obsessed by the war's outcome. My father had a huge map of the German army's progress, taken from a two-page spread in the *New York Times*, pinned to his bedroom wall. It was, indeed, the only decoration in his stark surroundings. I remember seeing the threatening black arrows cutting deep into the Russian countryside. I did not fully realize that these were places my father had known as a child, places in which he might still have friends and family.

My father did all that he could to help the war effort as a publisher. Having started his own tiny firm, he published—in French—books from the French resistance as soon as they began to appear. He published Louis Aragon's poetry and the wartime writings of his old friend Antoine de Saint Exupéry, who lived in New York for a while before he went back to fly for the Free French and eventually died in a crash while on a mission. Fiction works of the resistance gradually surfaced, and my father issued the first of these, *Les Silences de la mer* in New York, while the RAF dropped tiny microfilm editions of the book over France. The book had been written by someone using the nom de plume "Vercors," and my father had no idea who the author actually was. In their correspondence, he and Gide speculated, inaccurately, as to who he might be, going so far as to include Sartre among their suspects. (The actual author turned out to be the far less-known Jean Bruller.) It is amazing to think that this quiet narrative of a French family who refuse to talk to the German officer who is billeted with them should have seemed such a daring statement. Later, the resistance had far worse things to write about.

Next came Joseph Kessel's *L'Armée des ombres* and other books that were read by fellow exiles but made little impact on America. Gide sent his manuscripts from North Africa, not wishing them to be published in occupied France. My father published the latest installment of Gide's *Journals*, as well as his *Thésée*, a new translation of *Hamlet*, and a volume called *Imaginary Interviews*. Later he would publish several books by Jacques Maritain and Malraux's three-volume *The Pyschology of Art*. My father's list continued to grow and soon extended to Latin America, where translations of Gide's work began to appear in Argentina, thanks to Victoria Ocampo, the owner of the publishing house Sur, a mainstay of pro-French thought in that Fascist and pro-German country. My father's correspondence with Gide during these years is filled with the details of all this activity and of the contractual complications that came with the uncertain mail service and the other hazards of war.

For a while, after the invasion of North Africa, my father wrote to exiled intellectuals, including Raymond Aron, who were trying to start a cultural magazine from the world of the Free French, but those efforts came to naught. Still, in the U.S. and in England, where many of my father's books appeared in now-forgotten Penguin French editions, the books played a symbolic role in showing that there was more to France than Vichy's cowardice and complicity.

Still in all, the number of copies of books my father was able to sell was tiny, certainly not enough to live on. So it was a godsend that in 1944 he was able to join Pantheon Books, which had been founded by Kurt Wolff, the distinguished German famous for first publishing Franz Kafka and others, who was also in exile and with whom Jacques would work for the rest of his life. At Pantheon my father would continue to publish his French authors as well as design all the books, many of which won prizes for their classic simplicity and beauty. I would often visit his office in the lovely Georgian building on the south side of Washington Square, part of what was known as the "genius row" of houses where Henry

James and other artists and intellectuals had once lived . . . all of which were ruthlessly torn down by New York University for its law school in the hapless fifties.

* * *

After I'd spent two years in Montclair, my parents lamented my absence as much as I did and I finally came back to New York. The weekend visits had been insufficient for all of us, and so my parents enrolled me in a nearby public school. We had moved to Seventy-fifth Street because my parents thought it was in the catchment area for PS 6, then as now well known as a safe middle-class enclave within the school system. But my parents had miscalculated by a few blocks, and I found myself assigned to the Robert F. Wagner Public School instead. The area to the east of Third Avenue, with its endless rows of old-fashioned tenements, was still very much an Irish slum, and the school proved a dangerous place for me. Kids were eager to steal bikes, and I soon learned that "What time is it?" was a dangerous question if one possessed a watch. Each day my only Jewish classmate, Kenneth Silverman—now a famous biographer—and I were set upon by our classmates and soundly beaten for having killed their Christ. There was no defense against the relentless mob, and each day my mother caught me arriving home with a missing handful of hair. I never confessed to the problems but instead sought simply to come up with excuses for playing hooky. Clearly, my mother understood, making no objection to my frequent headaches and fevers. The next year, I was found a safe haven, a Quaker School on East Fifteenth Street called Friends Seminary.

The trip to Friends involved going sixty blocks, a half hour's ride, first on the trolley and then on the old elevated train, whose stations included the iron stoves immortalized in Berenice Abbott's photographs of New York in the thirties. No one worried about a ten-year-old's ability to negotiate public transport alone. I soon found myself in a far safer and more suitable environment. My mother, oblivious to the ways of New York, sent me off for my first day in carefully pressed gray flannel shorts and with a dab of cologne behind each ear. But while the boys in my class may have raised an eyebrow, the girls were all smitten and I received a bumper crop of Valentine's Day cards.

I was far from the only European refugee child in the school. There were many others, but we never noticed or talked about this. We were all firmly on the path to Americanization, and I realized only much later that, for example, in the class ahead of me was Clem Zimmer, the son of Heinrich Zimmer, a noted German expert on Indian art and philosophy. Another of his classmates was Christian Wolff, son of Helen and Kurt Wolff, who had taken my father on as their partner at Pantheon Books.

It was at Friends that I found myself truly fitting into the American mold. Though the place was very much an intellectual hothouse, it never occurred to me that we were anything but an average American high school. Did we not, after class, repair to a local coffee shop, just as Archie and Veronica did in the comics I so enjoyed?

The comics were my favorite reading and, subconsciously, a guide to what America was really like. In addition to reading children's books, from a very early age I had subscribed to Looney Tunes and the Disney comics. My annual dollar brought great pleasure to my mailbox every month. As I grew older, I graduated to more advanced narratives and found myself appreciating Joe Palooka, the somewhat dense boxer, who was a staunch defender of our war aims. It didn't occur to me that other children might not be as fascinated by the political subtext (although I'm sure I shared with many of my contemporaries their puzzlement at Superman's inability to do more for the war effort). After our victory, I was a great fan of Li'l Abner's Shmoos, those jovial creatures who were to bring us all the peace and plenty that we rightly expected from the postwar world. The children's books I read were at a much higher cultural level—a series of biographies of famous composers and classic favorites from Europe—but the comics led me into American popular culture, a world I met neither at home nor at school. I immersed myself happily.

So eager was I to obtain the newest comics that each Saturday night, I would walk up to Eighty-sixth Street and Lexington Avenue and buy all the Sunday papers that had comic supplements. There were four in those days, excluding the *Times* that my parents got at home every day. Then, I would take my cache of cartoons to a classic soda-fountain parlor called Addie Vallins, where I would treat myself to an old-fashioned American feast of a coffee ice cream sundae, complete with whipped cream, almonds, and a cherry. (Years later, when working with the great American folklorist Richard Dorsen, I asked where he wanted us to lunch, and he replied sheepishly that he'd been wondering if there was still a place in New York where one could find an ice cream sundae. He taught in Indiana and complained that soda fountains were no longer available in the heartland of America.

Happily, there was still one remaining soda parlor in Midtown, to which I took him.) After my session at Vallins, I would return home with my stack of newspapers. I gradually began to read the front sections as well, becoming the print addict that I remain to this day.

In those days, Eighty-sixth Street was the heart of Yorkville, then the German neighborhood, and in spite of the war I enjoyed visiting the area and even trying out my schoolboy German. Nowadays, Yorkville is as replete with sneaker and telephone stores as any suburban mall, but then it was filled with German restaurants, cafés, and other German businesses. In the 1940s, New York was still a European city in many ways. The Upper East Side uncannily duplicated the geography of the old Austro-Hungarian empire: The Germans were in Yorkville in the mid-Eighties neighborhood, the Austrians and the Hungarians huddled together in the upper Seventies, the Czechs were slightly to the south in the lower Seventies, and the Poles and Ukrainians were much farther to the south, on the Lower East Side. This meant that my mother and I could indulge ourselves in delicious Hungarian pastries at Mrs. Herbst's bakery a few blocks from our house, or at German pastry shops like Die Kleine Konditorei on Eighty-sixth Street.

The tastes of home are the classic form of nostalgia for immigrants, even those not as addicted to sweet treats as I was. On arriving in New York, my parents were delighted to discover an excellent Austrian chocolate store called Altman and Kuhn, which was on Fifth Avenue near Rockefeller Center. I remember those European delicacies as one of the rare treats that wartime New York could offer. Not long ago, while passing through

Vienna, I was amazed to see that Altman and Kuhn had returned to their birthplace. But when I tried to tell the salesclerks that I had known their New York incarnation, they assured me that none had ever existed.

As time passed, my links to Europe became more tenuous and increasingly gastronomic, due in part to my proximity to these European neighborhoods. But my real life increasingly centered on school, where I led a happy (and safe) existence. I became caught up in most aspects of American life, but no one at Friends seemed very interested in popular music or sports, so my own predilections seemed normal. There were plenty of classmates with whom I could have serious discussions, and we shared many of the same tastes in reading. The fact that I spoke French at home—and would never have dreamed of doing otherwise—did not seem unusual to me (although it would astonish my daughters, years later). My life was comfortably schizophrenic. Europe was in the distant past, and it never occurred to me that we might one day return.

But meanwhile, though I didn't realize it until much later, my parents thought every day about returning. Their daily existence was a very different thing from mine. Though I knew that our means were modest, I didn't realize how poor we were or what a contrast this presented to their previous life in Paris. At Pantheon during that time, neither my father nor the Wolffs earned more than $100 per week, enough in those days to pay our rent but not too much more. Still, in spite of our poverty, my parents tried hard to recreate their Paris social milieu. They were able to find a few friends, nearly all European, with some American exceptions, such as Meyer Schapiro, an art historian whose phenomenal knowledge of European culture made him an essential part of the exile community. I remember my father's evenings of discussion with Schapiro, Hannah Arendt, and others. The French, German, and Austrian exiles, such as the novelist Hermann Broch, felt very close. With Arendt, in part due to years of her Paris exile, my parents shared not only a common past, but the travails of their American existence. It would be many years before Arendt would find even the most modest of teaching posts; before that, she worked at part-time jobs with Jewish organizations and later for the German-exile publisher Schocken. Meanwhile, she could identify with my father, who had been close to several German publishers during the Weimar years. He had been good friends and shared projects with Harry Kessler, "the Red Count," who was one of the leading left-wing intellectuals of that time and a distinguished publisher. And although I can't recall it, I assume that my father spoke German with these friends. I never knew whether the language he spoke with Kurt Wolff at Pantheon was French or German, but it certainly wasn't English.

I was allowed to sit in on these evenings of talk, and it made me think that my parents were part of a vital and important intellectual world. But my father wrote bitterly to Gide about how few real friends he had in New York and how difficult it was to recreate a cultural life. He shared that difficulty with many of the French exiles who found New York very hard to get used to. Even as successful a fellow refugee as Max Ernst, then married to Peggy Guggenheim and living a luxurious life, would complain of a sense of loneliness and isolation, saying that "New York had no communal life, no cafés, no communication."[3] Curiously, various cultural histories suggest that the many German refugees in Los Angeles had a contrary complaint: They regretted that they saw each other all the time and barely met the natives. But the concentration of intellectuals and theatre people there was far greater than in New York, and in such a company town there were many occasions for people to work together and share one another's complaints about the Hollywood system.

Some of the few places in New York where my father found he could feel at home were the little Italian cafés behind Pantheon's offices on Washington Square. These were not the fancy espresso joints of later years, but tiny, barren, working-class storefronts, each with a coffee machine and a few linoleum-covered tables. But they sold very good, strong espresso and accepted anyone who wanted to join the game of gin rummy that the old Italian immigrants played all day long. I would often find Jacques there, happily playing cards during his lunch break.

After my father's death, I was shocked to see that among the few belongings he had managed to bring from Europe were his formal evening clothes. Clearly, on leaving France my parents had assumed that they would continue their prewar life, dressing for dinner at the houses of friends or for concerts. Though he would occasionally wear his old outfit, it was more a symbol of a lost world than an aide in the new one.

---

[3] Quoted in *Exiles and Émigrés: The Flight of European Artists from Hitler* (Los Angeles: Los Angeles County Museum of Art, 1997).

As the war ended, a stream of French people came to visit New York. I still have a photo of my parents dining with Jean-Paul Sartre on his now-famous visit, which was the first time they met. Much publicized by both the American and French papers, Sartre was one of a group brought over by the State Department to discover their ally and the French exiles. Though Sartre made a point in his writings that those who had escaped France could never understand what life during the Occupation had been like, he seemed willing enough to spend an evening with them and to travel around the country as a would-be reporter. Still, though he would later write his famous essay *Anti-Semite and Jew*, the fact that some people, like my parents, had fled because of a very real threat did not seem to occur to him, and he apparently shared the feeling with many of those who had stayed behind that it was they who had suffered terribly, while the refugees had had an easy time of it.

Many others were less critical of the exiles and eager to see the city, and their itinerary became a routine: Jazz in Harlem on Saturday night followed by a walk through the deserted canyons of Wall Street on Sunday morning. My parents enjoyed guiding the visitors around the town and renewing their own links to Paris life, but it added to their feelings of frustration at not being able to go back—partly because of my father's ill health—as they had assumed they would the moment the war ended. Living out their lives in the United States had never been their expectation. The war had been a painful parenthesis, not a permanent move to a new country. Nearly all of the French exiles were looking forward to returning as soon as possible. Claude Lévi-Strauss, in his memoir *Near and Far*, writes about the different attitudes of his colleagues in the exile university they had created in New York's

New School. "Those who considered themselves completely French had but one idea, to return to France and take up their jobs. The others, more recently naturalized, were unsure as to what their fate would be."[4] Many of the other exiles worried that they would no longer have the jobs they had left. This would, in fact, turn out to be Jacques' situation. Once the template of the Pléiade had been established, it was relatively easy for Gallimard to continue the series without him and, although Gallimard had had to reinstate his profit-sharing contract to make up for the war years, they decided that this did not entail offering him his job back. Sartre was far more brutal when questioned by the OSS during his visit in 1945 when he said, "Not a single exile failed to ask... with the greatest apprehension whether they would be looked down upon when they returned. It's much worse, they've been forgotten."[5]

Our German friends, understandably, had a different feeling. Very few, if any, were willing to go back. In spite of the difficulties, they now felt that they were American, and even going back to visit was often painful. Knowing that they would not return must have helped them to become more American. Many of the Marxist theoreticians found themselves accommodating to the American scene, and to the marketplace. The great Bauhaus architects stopped thinking about workers' housing and began to design the office buildings for which they became rightly famous. Gropius and Mies van der Rohe became part of

---

[4] Quoted in Emmanuelle Loyer, *Paris à New York* (Paris: Grasset, 2005), 344, which also details my father's work in New York.
[5] Ibid., 348.

the American landscape, literally as well as figuratively. Only a few of the very famous, such as the members of the Frankfurt School, were lured back with prestigious university posts. None of my German schoolmates' families considered the possibility of returning, though they had been important figures in the Weimar cultural landscape.

Happily involved in my new school life, I was unaware of my parents' feeling of isolation and their desire to return as soon as possible. It never occurred to me that this might be an option, much less their cherished dream. It was only much later, on reading those letters home, that I realized the full extent of their exile, and their pain.

By the time I was thirteen, I felt that I had been thoroughly Americanized. I was persuaded that I belonged in my new country and no longer had any interest in the birthplace I had left a mere seven years before. I fit perfectly into the classic immigrant pattern of assimilation. I assumed that I was a typical American teenager, though in fact I was very far from being one—sports bored me and I felt no attraction toward popular music. But other aspects of America fascinated me, particularly the American political scene.

Nineteen forty-eight was my first real presidential campaign, and I was determined to comprehend it thoroughly. No one thought it the slightest bit odd that a thirteen-year-old would be interested enough to come to each campaign headquarters and ask for their party platforms, position papers, and, of course, campaign buttons. The poorer parties asked if I'd be willing to stay on and work as a volunteer. Politics was still a labor-intensive activity and everyone depended on those willing to spend endless hours in their storefront headquarters, stapling, mimeographing, and handing out leaflets. (Years later the New York Democratic leader Herman Badillo lamented to me the degree to which money had replaced the local storefronts. As he explained it, a candidate's first task used to be to round up a few beautiful women who could be seen through the plate-glass window. Subsequently, enough young men would then volunteer and the core of a workforce was assured.)

The 1948 election, as it turned out, was an ideal introduction to American politics in its most wide-ranging possibilities. There were liberal Democrats and conservative Republicans, and more: While the Republicans had united behind Tom Dewey, the Democrats were not exactly unanimous in their support of President Harry Truman. The Southern racist Democrats—the so-called Dixiecrats—had splintered off to Truman's right and were fronting their own candidate, Strom Thurmond. Meanwhile, FDR's former vice president, Henry Wallace, and his Progressive Party had splintered off to Truman's left. Even further to the left was Norman Thomas, running, as usual, as a Socialist, even if only symbolically. So, for the last time in modern American history, there had been an extremely wide range of choices across the political spectrum.

I knew I was for the Socialist candidate Norman Thomas, because I had decided I was a Socialist, and also because I knew I was against Wallace, the Progressive party candidate and *New Republic* magazine editor. He seemed too pro-Communist for my taste. It didn't occur to me that my socialism came from reading Léon Blum rather than Thomas. After all, this was supposed to be an international creed.

But I was realistic enough to know that it was Truman that I wanted to win, which at the time seemed highly unlikely. Everyone seemed certain of Dewey's victory. (In an attempt to teach me the follies of gambling, my father bet me that Dewey would win, giving me odds of one hundred to one. After a day spent watching the vote-counting in increasing disbelief, I gleefully collected his twenty-five very unexpected dollars late on the day after the election.) But I knew that my heart belonged to the phantom Socialist Party, still headed by Thomas. After the Soviet coup d'état in Czechoslovakia and the murder of the Czech leader Jan Masaryk, I felt one had to stand both for Socialism and Democracy.

My father watched bemused—pleased that I was so interested in American politics, but worried by my total chauvinism. It was time, he felt, that I should discover what the rest of the world was like by making a return visit to France. Both my parents were eager for me to go back and meet our friends and relatives and get some idea of what had been left behind. In a letter to Gide, dated May 23, 1949, my father described what to expect when he met me: a boy whose main interests, in addition to collecting stamps, was "politics. He takes in an enormous quantity of newspapers, magazines, all sorts of political books. He listens to the radio. Better informed about current affairs, both foreign and domestic, than your average Congressman. Never bored. Likes being by himself and clearly prefers the company of adults." My father was also worried about my reluctance to read French. (As for Gide's own books, he thought it better to have me read them later, when I was older and would be more likely to understand them.)

My father himself was still desperate to return. Going back to his old publishing job in Paris was impossible, and his increasingly frail health—his worsening emphysema—made the Midi far more attractive to him than New York; his dream was to go back to the South of France, where I was headed to visit André Gide and Roger Martin du Gard, and open a bookstore. But his friends in France discouraged these hopes, saying that a bookstore was an unlikely venture. Martin du Gard and Gide wrote to each other about this, unbeknownst to my father, just before I left to visit them. As Martin du Gard's letter put it,

> *Should we encourage him to return to this absurd Europe? And specially to France? And specially to Nice? What will he do there? What bitter bread awaits him? . . . Schiffrin's only real skill, and I believe it's very great, is in publishing. But in Nice that is out of the question. A bookstore? But there have been thirty new ones since '45 and they are all stagnating, not only like everywhere else, but even more than elsewhere. . . . In Nice people buy digests and movie magazines. I think it very dangerous to encourage him.*

Martin du Gard's letters to my father were even more discouraging. In May, 1945, he wrote urging Jacques not to give in to his nostalgia for the past:

> *Europe is finished. There are only ruins. Distress is so widespread that between the discouragement of the victors and that of the vanquished, there is only a question of degrees. At this time, there is the slow return of the survivors of the torture camps, those specters escaped from Hell who are now strangers. . . . There is a stifling atmosphere, which paralyzes all* joie de vivre, *all attempts at hope.*

Two years later, in January, 1947, he continued to try to dissuade my father from thinking of coming back.

> *You have no idea how sad Paris is, how depressing, worn out. . . You would find us all aged by twenty-five years. We have not completely lost the feeling of being an occupied country. . . The passivity of the French remains for me a source of inexhaustible horror.*

(Other observers agreed. In the *New Yorker*, Janet Flanner wrote from Paris in March, 1947, that "there has been a climate of indubitable and growing malaise in Paris." George Kennan wrote in a report to the State Department at the same time that Europe was affected by a "profound exhaustion of physical plant and spiritual vigor."[6])

But Martin du Gard and Gide could have saved their arguments. I now realize that there was really no possibility of my father being able to return; they did not realize how ill he was. His emphysema had worsened to the point that he needed to have an oxygen tank by his bedside, something that would have been extremely difficult if not impossible to arrange in the still-austere climate of postwar France.

So my parents had differing motives for sending me back, none of which I realized. They wanted me to rediscover France, but at the same time I was something of an advance guard, feeling out the territory to see what it would be like there for all of us. Later I realized that I had been like the dove sent from Noah's ark to see what life was left after the flood.

---

[6] Both quoted by Tony Judt in *Postwar* (New York: Penguin Press, 2005).

The trip was planned with the most modest of budgets, $50, meant to cover expenses for the entire two-month visit. There was no question of my staying in a hotel, even for a single night, nor of our paying for the crossing. We would depend entirely on our friends and family: My parents had friends in New York's French community who worked for the huge French grain exporting company Louis Dreyfus, and they were able to find me a free bunk on a small freighter.

My mother escorted me to the Philadelphia harbor, from which the ship was to depart. There, we confronted my ocean liner, a small ten-thousand ton freighter carrying Marshall Plan coal to France—the kind of vessel called a "liberty ship" during the war, when they were the major form of transport. It contained one passenger cabin—a minuscule space with two bunks—which I would share with a twenty-year-old French college student returning from a year in America. Neither he nor the crew seemed surprised to find a thirteen-year-old alone onboard. The ship's officers with whom I took my meals were certainly not inhibited by my presence when it came to discussing their memories of all the whores they had met in their travels. I remember particularly vividly the story of a Brazilian woman who turned the Virgin's image to the wall when she settled down to work.

The crossing took three weeks. Our speed, I was told, was the equivalent of a bicyclist's, some fifteen miles per hour, whereas the great ocean liners sped along at sixty mph. We chugged along uneventfully, until one evening we suddenly heard the strains of a lively waltz crossing the ocean. I thought at first that it was my imagination, but then I realized that it couldn't be; everyone else had heard it as well. All too quickly an explanation hove into view.

Close to us—all too close—was the *Queen Mary.* The waltzes were coming from the ship's orchestra and their nightly ball. It was an apparition out of Fellini's *Amarcord,* but a far more dangerous one; we were tossed around mercilessly by the massive waves caused by the enormous liner's passage. We had no time to enjoy the music, clinging to the rails for dear life as the gigantic ship bore on, finally leaving us bobbing listlessly in its wake.

Shortly before we landed, the student and I were told that our destination was being changed to the port of Brest, and I thought I had better send a cable home. Mindful of the expense, I kept it to as few words as possible: "Brest, love." But I could have saved the money, since we landed not in Brest after all but instead in Caen. Thus, my first look at Europe was a shocking one: Caen had been badly bombed in 1944 during the liberation, and even by the time of my landing five years later it was still largely in utter ruin. The area around the port was completely flattened, and the town center had very few buildings standing. I hadn't expected anything like this. The American press had given no indication that Europe was still so shattered. I proceeded through the devastation to the Paris train, badly shaken by this first view of what the war had meant to France.

Still, this did not inhibit the youthful American chauvinist in me. Indeed, it encouraged and confirmed my feelings of American superiority. The other passengers in my crowded eight-person train compartment seemed the ideal audience for my diatribe on the importance to them of the Marshall Plan and of America's generosity. (The Plan had indeed greatly helped France's economy to recover, but many of the French were reluctant to admit this.) Nor could I resist a short lecture on the value of the American way of life—the higher wages, higher standard of living, and God knows what other details—that must have infuriated my fellow passengers. Amazing that they all withstood the urge to throw me out of a train window.

My arrival in Paris was similar in some ways to my arrival in Caen. Unlike London, which had lost an incredible 3.5 million dwellings, central Paris had been largely untouched by bombs (though the outlying factories had been frequent targets); however, the city, though still beautiful, seemed worn and impoverished. People on the busses and in the Metro were poorly dressed and did indeed smell as if they rarely bathed, as in the crude clichés that still fill American guidebooks.

The apartment where I stayed looked as if it, too, had undergone a harsh war. My father had asked his old friends Louis and Simone Martin-Chauffier to put me up, which they did with great kindness. They probably had no idea that though they lived in a grand building near the Trocadero on the Avenue Georges Mandel, their home seemed incredibly shabby and run-down to my American eyes. Their apartment seemed empty to me, with little furniture, peeling walls, and bare lights. Louis had been a leading Communist journalist before the war and as such had been deported to the concentration camp Dachau, in which he had barely survived the war years. In many ways, his apartment reflected his own appearance: He was tired, worn out, having never recovered from his Calvary. One of the first things I did upon my return to New York was to read his memoir, and then all the others that I could find, such as David Rousset's classic but now forgotten *The Other Kingdom*, Primo Levi's *If This is a Man*, and the others that described the experience that could so easily have been my family's. These are books that haunt me to this day.

Impoverished by the war as they were, they still employed a maid, and Louis was back at work as a journalist, still very much a committed Communist. He took me to the July 14 Bastille Day celebration, which for years was the annual focal point of the Party's recruiting efforts. I sat next to him proudly in the grandstand reviewing a seemingly unending parade. I don't remember feeling any more tenderly toward Henry Wallace and his Communist backers as a result, but later my father wrote to Gide that he feared my visit had made me much more critical of America than he had previously thought possible. But then, any contact with reality would have had to have some impact on the boilerplate chauvinism I had brought with me to France.

Although my parents had not suggested precisely what I should do, my weeks in Paris were spent exactly as they would have wished. I wrote them enthusiastic letters, describing the city as "heavenly beautiful" despite the war-weary atmosphere. I wanted to see it all and acted from some subconscious desire to rediscover—or indeed discover—the city we had left. I had bought one of the small red pocket atlases that every Parisian owns, which shows the city in each of its twenty *arrondissements*, and I left every morning intending to walk through one of them. By the end of my trip, I had covered most of the city and seen most of its monuments and museums and other highlights, including the supposedly sinful areas around the Pigalle that intrigued my adolescent hormones.

I also realized that other appetites could be more easily satisfied: The famous *patisserie*, Carette's, was nearby on the Trocadero, and it was there during one of my strolls that I discovered the marvels of French confectioneries. (I passed by the spot recently; the place is still there, but I hesitated to try their Café

Liègois, a concoction very much like an ice cream sundae of old, which was my first sublime gastronomic experience in Paris—my Proustian Madeleine. I was sure that no modern version could live up to that exquisite memory.) On another occasion, one of my father's sisters, Bella, and her husband Serge, took me to Les Halles, at the time still a wholesale food market whose vast glass pavilions housed veritable walls of food. I encountered there for the first time a phalanx of wild strawberries giving off an over-whelming scent. If they made an actual perfume from this smell, I told my aunt, I would marry the first woman who wore it.

Next to the Martin-Chauffier's apartment on the Trocadero was the Palais de Chaillot, a complex of museums and theatres. On several evenings I went to see performances of the TNP, the famous Théâtre National Populaire, which was run by Jean Vilar. His aim was to reach the broadest possible audience, and his group reached out to factory workers and others who would never have gone to a play otherwise. The atmosphere in the theatre itself was electric and joyous, and I was very impressed by this suc-cessful attempt to bring culture to the masses, just as had been done in the U.S. in the thirties by Clifford Odets and others in the New Deal's theatre groups. Vilar's success stayed in the back of my mind, and I am sure it affected the way I thought when I finally began to work at NAL, the mass-market house where I got my first publishing job a few years later.

I was also amused to ride Paris' lovely old busses with the open back platforms. I noted the enamel plaques above every row of seats. They specified that windows would be opened or closed each morning according to prevailing meteorological conditions, and that if a dispute arose over this, final authority rested with those nearest the window. (A shorter version is still to be seen on the busses today.) I was astonished to see that a country that had just survived a period of unparalleled criminality, with the state itself as the leading culprit, could maintain prewar injunctions about civility and avoiding unnecessary conflict. I wonder how often those signs were obeyed.

In any event, not all my time in Paris was spent on sightseeing and other purely pleasurable activities. There were some business visits to carry out. My father had asked me to visit Gallimard, the publishing house to whom he had sold his Pléiade series and where he had worked during his last years in France. After the war, of course, he had hoped to return to his old job, but the Gallimards had filled his position and made clear that there would be no room for him. So my visit was, at best, delicate and fraught.

As I wrote to my parents after the visit, I found the firm "very rich, full of Gallimards but very businesslike, very cold and very sad. I shook lots of hands, everyone asked how my father was, but it's impossible to tell you whether they were really interested or just being polite."

On the surface, at least, Gaston Gallimard, the firm's founder and probably the most famous publisher in France, had, despite the circumstances, maintained cordial relations with my father. He was well along in years and must have thought it unusual to find himself in a *tête-à-tête* with a boy who'd just turned fourteen. In any case, he invited me to lunch in his apartment and did so very kindly. I can remember no awkward pauses in our conversation, although I should note that my father had not told me of the series of problems that had started when Gallimard had dismissed him a mere nine years before. Nor had he discussed with me how he felt about the resumption of relations with Gallimard after the war, when my father had still hoped to return to Paris and his old job.

The history was a complicated one: As soon as the Germans had occupied Paris, they locked the doors at Gallimard, and the Gallimard family and staff, my father included, headed for the countryside. Gaston was eager to start publishing again and was willing to accept the Nazi conditions under which he could do so. This involved firing the firm's two Jews, my father and the sales director, Louis-Daniel Hirsch; allowing Nazi-appointed editors to enter the firm; and agreeing to hand over the editorship of the firm's famous journal, *La Nouvelle Revue Française*, which had been started decades before by Gide. Otto Abetz, the German ambassador, had spent many years in prewar France and knew the cultural scene perfectly. He realized the importance of Gallimard and *La Nouvelle Revue Française*. Having both continue would give the impression that French culture was going on as before. Abetz cleverly chose a well-regarded Fascist author, Pierre Drieu de la Rochelle, as the new *Nouvelle Revue* editor and, with him firmly in charge, Gallimard was allowed to continue publishing, within the very carefully delineated Nazi policies.

Gallimard, the man and the company, had also been under attack from the French Fascists, who were often more extreme in their language than the very sophisticated Germans. Indeed, the Germans often used the Fascists throughout the Occupation both to apply pressure on Vichy from forces to their right and, ultimately, to conduct murderous attacks on the Resistance. Writing in *Au Pilori* on October 18, 1940, Paul Riche denounced Gallimard and its books:

> *Down with the books of Gide, Malraux, Aragon, Freud, the*
> *surrealist books—the pacifist books, the anti-Nazis—which*
> *have troubled the relations between Europe [i.e., Germany]*
> *and France. . . . How many Jewish names there are at*
> *Gallimard—Freud, Benda, Schiffrin—Gallimard is eager*
> *to return to Paris, already the blacks and nigger-lovers are*
> *waiting for him . . . .*[7]

Et cetera. Faced with such attacks, one can well imagine Gaston's relief at being offered the chance to continue publishing, even at the cost of firing some of his best employees and letting the Germans take over his flagship journal. And it must be added in all fairness that many publishers acted far worse than Gallimard. Some were enthusiastically pro-Nazi and anti-Semitic and published accordingly. One hurriedly offered to pulp their translations of Heine, the German Jewish classic poet, even before the Germans banned his work. Others were quick to obey Abetz's subsequent list of censored titles, the infamous *Liste Otto*, which forbade the sale of hundreds of titles by Jewish, anti-Nazi, and Marxist authors.

I became more keenly aware of all this many years later when I read the excellent *History of French Publishing Under the Occupation*, by Pascal Fouché, a history largely forgotten by most Frenchmen. But I was largely unaware of all this when I found myself visiting Gaston Gallimard's grand apartment. It was in the Palais Royale, one of the most beautiful squares in Paris: There was a vast arcade surrounding a park featuring three avenues of near-identical trees, which created a leafy arcade that matched

---

[7] Hebey, 132.

that of the building. The building's arcade was no longer the home of prostitutes and gamblers as described by Balzac in *Lost Illusions,* but rather featured one wing of government offices, another three wings containing sumptuous shops and restaurants, and luxurious apartments above. It seemed incredible to me that mere mortals could live there overlooking such splendor. Even Gallimard himself seemed impressed, and pointed out to me Colette's apartment across the gardens. I had not yet read any of her work but knew enough to be impressed myself. (Not that I was completely unaware of her. She played an important role in our family legend. She had once invited my mother, then a young woman, to her house for the weekend. On being shown her room, Simone found that the floor had been covered with rose petals. Nothing further happened as far as I know, but as I grew old enough to go on dates, I felt that I could never live up to this standard of seduction.)

By the end of my month, I felt that I had taken possession of Paris once again. I had seen where my father had worked. I had also seen the Rue de l'Université, where we had lived until the Germans seized our apartment. I had gone back to the Tuileries and seen the merry-go-round that I remembered clearly, and to the Luxembourg Gardens, where the boat pond was exactly as I remembered it. I had walked down the dreary grand boulevards and visited the stamp market off the Rond Point of the Champs-Élysées. I had seen the relatives who had returned to Paris at the war's end and begun their lives anew. They had fled to the South and had, for the most part, survived Vichy's attacks on French Jews—except for my aunt Bella's mother, who had refused to go into hiding and had been deported to a concentration camp, where she was killed. The others had managed to live but had lost most of their possessions and were living lives of relative poverty. My uncle Simon, alone among them all, had been able to return from America and take back his old house—partly looted by his neighbors as was so often the case during the war. Elisabeth Gille, daughter of the writer Irène Némirovsky, in *Shadows of a Childhood,* her own wartime memoir that I published, tells of going back to their old apartment and finding their belongings, including her toys, in the concierge's apartment. It was all too common an experience. In our own case, the Germans had been far more meticulous. After the war, we heard from some army official that a case of our books had been retrieved in Vienna, carefully labeled as having been taken from our apartment. We were able to reclaim these and my father had, in his final few years, the chance to see again some of the earliest books that he had published.

In spite of all of this, of the memories of expropriation and exile, I nonetheless felt some ownership of the city, some feeling of what it was like to live there.

I was ready, then, for the next part of the trip, which was to the Midi to visit Gide.

* * *

Gide by then was one of my father's oldest and closest friends. They had met in Paris in 1922, shortly after my father's arrival and his decision to launch his original series of Russian classics with Pushkin's *The Queen of Spades.* As was common at the time, my father had been taught French from the earliest days of his Russian childhood, and so he decided to translate the book himself.

Nonetheless, he also decided to seek someone to help him check and improve his translation, and, out of the blue, he wrote to Gide, who was already very famous. From their published correspondence we can trace the way their relationship developed from that first contact.

They did not, at the outset, seem to have much in common, except for their love of language and literature. But that core love flourished as they began to translate together. Many of the works my father had rendered from the Russian had never been translated directly into French before. Much of what was available had not been translated into French from the original Russian text but rather retranslated from Constance Garnett's famous English translations. Together, my father and Gide discovered the many affinities between French and Russian. But their earliest letters give only a glimpse of the budding relationship between the two men. It is interesting to note how much attention was paid by both of them to the tiniest of technical details, such as correcting typographical errors, making sure that title pages gave appropriate credit, and the like. Meanwhile, in reading Gide's *Journals,* one can see the personal friendship forming—the dinners together, the films they saw after a day's work, the shared working vacations planned as a week but extending into a fortnight as both men corrected manuscripts and galleys.

Still, the differences between them must at first have seemed daunting. In an early letter to a friend, Gide comments on my father's "Semitic" ways. Even on hearing of my father's death many years later, Gide was to comment that he had been "the only Jew he ever really liked." And the last of their collected letters has my father scolding Gide for anti-Semitic comments he had made about literature. In addition to their letters, some of Gide's *Journals* show that the issue troubled him, although his ideas seemed unchanged. In his *Journals,* on January 8, 1948, he wrote that he had been reading Sartre's essay on anti-Semitism:

> *Am a bit disappointed… his thesis is the same one that was argued by my friend Schiffrin. The Jews' most common characteristics (by this I mean those that you, the anti-Semites, criticize them for) are those acquired over the centuries, those which you have forced them to assume, etc. The long conversation which I had with him reminds me of certain arguments which no longer surprise me. They seem to be today more clever and specious than correct, in spite of the profound and tender affection that I have always had, and now evermore, for Schiffrin; in whom, I must say in addition, I see very few of what one can consider as Jewish faults, but only their qualities. I feel the same about Léon Blum, for whom my esteem (and why not say my admiration) has only grown over the many years of our friendship….*

My father's last letter to Gide was, in fact, a long continuation of this debate. Clearly Gide never abandoned his stereotypes. But the penultimate line in his diaries, from November 11, 1950, concerns the news of my father's death. He would write to Justin O'Brien, the American editor of his diaries, about how disturbed he was by the news, and about how much he had liked my father.[8]

---

[8] Gide, *Journals.*

Still, to be fair, Gide's attitude about Jews was very common among the authors of his time. Many were far worse. A remarkable recent book, *La Nouvelle Revue Française des années sombres, 1940-41*, by Pierre Hebey, quotes the depressing list of authors who spoke ill of the Jews and, far worse, objected to Prime Minister Léon Blum's policy of welcoming refugees from Nazi Germany (just as did so many American politicians). The list is a veritable pantheon of French authors of the period, including such famous figures as Jean Giraudoux and Georges Bernanos and, even further to the right, Drieu de la Rochelle, Robert Brasillach, and Céline went much further than that. Brasillach wrote in the Vichy press, asking why certain named individuals had not yet been arrested (for which he was shot after the war—rightly, I feel). Céline complained to the German author Ernst Junger, at the time a German officer, that he was astonished that the Germans had not shot, hanged, and otherwise exterminated the Jews.[9] Perhaps most telling is a story that the now-revered Jean Cocteau blithely included in the postwar edition (Gallimard, 1989) of his diaries for 1942-44: When a Jew complains to him about having to wear the yellow star, Cocteau answers, "Don't worry, after the war you can make us wear false noses."[10] Cocteau, who had lived comfortably with the German occupants, going to their parties and receptions, apparently thought well enough of his *bon mot* to include the story without even realizing what it says about him.

So, Gide's comments, unfortunate as they are, are mild compared to even the most liberal of these others, and tempered by

---

[9] Hebey, 55.
[10] Noted in Hebey, 49.

the fact that he was obviously troubled by them. Once the Germans had conquered France, he was soon targeted by the collaborationists as a major villain, responsible for France's moral decay and therefore its defeat. He realized very early on what Pétain and Vichy stood for, and after giving in to Gallimard's pleas to write for Drieu de la Rochelle's journal, refused after a first anodyne contribution. He then decided not to publish his books in wartime France, and sent them instead to my father in New York. But Gide did much more than transcend the prejudice that was so common in his generation in France. He helped my father as a true friend, and was indeed responsible for the most important change in his publishing life. Gide had been crucial in arranging for my father to merge the Pléiade with Gallimard. Gide's diaries are full of mentions of the early Pléiade volumes, which he loved and carried with him. And it was Gide who began the talks with Gaston Gallimard. It took two years, Gide later explained, to persuade Gaston. Finally, in 1932, the Pléiade became part of the Gallimard firm; Jacques would remain in charge of the series and would be paid a royalty on each copy sold. (It would provide him with a comfortable income until the war. After the war, however, he felt that Gallimard had shortchanged him on the sales that had continued after his departure. He wrote Gallimard in vain about this.)

Gide was also eager to have my father accompany him on his famous trip to the USSR in 1936. The Soviets were, understandably, reluctant to allow entrée to an émigré such as my father—someone who could translate for Gide and help him to fully comprehend what was happening there. As the letters show, it took a while, but Gide was eventually able to persuade the Russians to allow my father to join him. Once there, Gide was surrounded by enthusiastic and admiring crowds, given the place of honor at the funeral of Maxim Gorky, even seated next to Stalin on various state occasions. He was fed endless and lavish banquets, while ordinary Russians had barely enough to buy their daily bread. Throughout, my father was able to translate what people were saying, which was often starkly contradictory to the official Party line.

The trip led to Gide's famous break with Communism, and after the trip, he spent long hours together with my father discussing whether his resultant critique of Russia, *Return from the USSR*, should appear during what would turn out to be the crucial final months of the Spanish Civil War. Gide had gotten a copy of his manuscript to Malraux on the Spanish front, and Malraux joined my father in urging Gide to hold off from publication, for fear that the book would weaken the already faltering international support for the Spanish Republicans. By then, the Russians were the Republic's main source of arms and support; criticizing them would automatically seem to favor Franco and his allies.

Nonetheless, Gide went ahead with the publication—and became the target of Communist hatred for years to come. Even after the Second World War, the leading Communist writer Louis Aragon and others tried unfairly to tar him with the collaborator's brush.

What is little reported is that despite his break with the Communists, Gide did all he could to defend the Spanish Republicans, working for months to create an international committee in their defense, trying to mobilize opinion against Franco's plans to kill many of those he had vanquished.

A few years later, in 1940, when my father was fired by Gallimard and our apartment behind the Chamber of Deputies—the Palais Bourbon—was seized by the Germans (its location was perfect for use by the occupying authorities), Gide lent my father the money that he needed to leave the country. The Occupation had many costs, but one that is rarely mentioned is simply the amount of money needed to survive the loss of home and income. The cost of living in hotels, crossing the frontier to the South, and surviving day to day quickly used up what little money we had. Gide literally saved our lives by getting us money, some of which he had to borrow. And then there was his intervening with Varian Fry, and his help keeping us out of the internment camps in Casablanca.

* * *

My parents had shielded me from much of this, and at the time I left Paris for the Midi I had only vague memories of our stay in Casablanca. I knew Gide as a great friend of our family. Even as a child I wrote to him frequently, dictating letters to my father, thanking him for presents he'd sent, and remembering our visits to his family home in Cuverville, where he had told me I could consider the small kid goat he kept there as mine. I'd never had a pet before, and this was a memorable thrill.

Gide was staying in a house lent to him by Florence J. Gould, an American millionaire, in Juan-les-Pins, a little town just outside of Antibes. Juan-les-Pins proved to be a very hot and dusty village, filled with opulent villas but not much to interest a jaded New Yorker. My biggest thrill was to find one of the first new French snack bars, a chain with the unlovely name of Pam Pam, where I could buy a sickly-sweet orangeade. The place seemed more appropriate to a teenager than the classic French café. But downtown Juan-les-Pins seemed a drag after Paris, and I spent much of my time in Gide's villa and its surrounding garden.

Gide had asked me to bring something from New York: a copy of a book by a young author about whom he'd been hearing good things. So, in my suitcase was a copy of *Other Voices, Other Rooms,* Truman Capote's first book. The back cover was adorned with a photo of Capote reclining on a divan like an odalisque in a tattersall vest, a photo that would become as famous as the book itself, and I now suspect it was this as much as the text that had intrigued Gide.

Life in the vast and sun-filled villa was appealing, though relatively formal and slow-paced. Gide had been ill the previous year and he still moved cautiously. Nonetheless he worked much of the day, in a huge office facing a lovely back garden. To my amazement, he answered all of the many letters he received. His journals, though, speak of his fatigue and his concern with his impending death, and he was indeed to die two years later, a year after my father. He kept those cares private, however. In daily life he seemed caught up in his work and his relationships. Certainly he was attentive and very kind with me, asking me questions about our life, about my visit to France so far. His letters back to my parents about me could not have been more enthusiastic or flattering. But there was a certain bemused distance in his attitude, friendly as he was. His time was also filled by the presence of others: He was surrounded by a number of handsome young admirers, friends who shared his daily life and our communal meals, all addressing him as *cher maître*. It was a phrase I found too embarrassing to use, and what to call him became the only truly awkward aspect of my stay. "Monsieur Gide" was impossible, as was "André." I spent my time there seeking some alternative to "Hey, you" and trying to circumnavigate the omnipresent honorifics.

No such problem presented itself when I took the bus from Juan les Pins to Nice to spend a day with another of my father's close friends, Roger Martin du Gard. Here, too, was someone I knew mainly as a family friend; I hadn't yet read any of his work, though later I would fall in love with *Les Thibault*, his multivolume saga of French life before and after the First World War, for which he won the Nobel Prize for literature.

Martin du Gard was very different from Gide, warm and friendly and very approachable, known for his welcoming smile and total lack of hauteur. In Nice we walked for hours along the Promenade des Anglais, talking like equals and having a marvelous time together. He seemed determined to show me every aspect of Nice, its harbor and still-lovely old town. The walk was nothing for me—I was used to crossing Paris by then—and of course it didn't occur to me that Martin du Gard was by then an old man. I felt I'd met a true friend. (Back in New York, I looked happily for the corncob pipes that he loved but could no longer find in France. Sending them was an inadequate way of showing how much our meeting had meant to me. His letters to my parents confirmed that the enjoyment had been mutual. Much later I learned Gide had offered him sympathy about the exhausting walk I'd imposed on him.)

My time in Juan-les-Pins was limited by the fact that Gide needed to go to the Avignon Festival for the premier of one of his plays, *Pasiphaé*. I moved on to spend a month with my mother's younger sister, Paulette, in the nearby town of Marmande. The Festival was then a very new thing, only in its second year. Gide's premiere would be a major event.

As we prepared for the long car ride, I noticed that everyone had been transformed. Gone were the informal summer clothes. All the young men were wearing extremely fashionable suits, and Gide was in his classic cape-overcoat and floppy, large-brimmed hat. I wore the suit that my uncle had bought me for the trip at Bonds, the cheap clothing store on Times Square known for the artificial waterfall atop its building that advertised a free second pair of trousers with every suit. I had never been very interested in fashion and paid no attention to my clothes, but suddenly I became aware of the stark contrast between the others in the party and my own shabby appearance. If Marshall Plan assistance had been merited at this point, it would have been needed in the opposite direction.

We set off in the early morning and at lunchtime pulled up before a vast roadside restaurant—not at all a simple café, but a very fancy place with dozens of tables stretching down through a huge space. At the opposite end, a good city block away, was the sole occupied table—a large lunch party which, even at this distance, one couldn't help overhear. The dominant voice was loud, raspy, and commanding, and belonged, I was told, to the eminent Catholic writer François Mauriac, a frequent critic of Gide's. Gide turned to his entourage and in a stage whisper said to us, "Can we pretend that we haven't seen them?" But the snub would have been considered scandalous and cooler heads soon prevailed; Gide was talked into leading our party across the restaurant to make appropriately polite greetings.

Later, at Avignon, the performance in the vast stone courtyard of the Palace of the Popes was dramatic and impressive. I had never seen such a setting, and the presentation stunned everyone. Gide was mobbed by admirers, all calling him *cher maître*, and I could see how such adulation could both please and alienate him. He seemed distant from ordinary mortals, and I had an inkling that his shyness and aloofness were in part a response to all this— something that, I would later learn, Martin du Gard had commented upon in their correspondence. However, this was the first time I had seen him in the role of Great Man, and later, when I had gone off to spend the end of my visit with my mother's family, I wrote home describing the Avignon event in great detail. I knew my parents hoped I would appreciate Gide's work and his place in French letters, so I composed as lavishly praising a missive as I could muster, hoping to fulfill their hopes for my visit.

Once I was back in New York, I plunged into my schoolboy's routine, eventually apologizing to Gide for the lateness of my thank-you letter by explaining how busy I'd been. Once again, I was an entirely American teenager, although my father wrote to Gide complaining that I had become much more critical of the U.S.

Knowing nothing of my father's hopes, I had no assumptions about our returning permanently to France. And given our poverty, I didn't think that I would ever vacation there again, either. It was only after college, when I won a scholarship to Cambridge, that I would again be able to visit Paris. Nor, in my wildest dreams, did I ever envisage the possibility of returning every year, as I was to do during my decades as a publisher. Instead, that first trip back seemed, quite simply, a self-contained event... not something that would lead to a life of divided loyalties.

When I returned from France, I found myself, if anything, increasingly fascinated by American politics.

Seeing that Europeans could be much more critical of the U.S. had intrigued me but hadn't changed my basic assumptions. I had formulated my politics when I was twelve, and by the time I got to France I was all too set in my ways. The 1948 presidential election had been, as mentioned, my first immersion in the underlying debates about American democracy that were all around me. From then on I had read the papers more avidly than ever, argued with my schoolmates, and was entirely absorbed in trying to figure out what was happening to our country and what our future would be.

The political milieu to which I returned had been intensified by the War, which had made each day's news seem more immediate. But it was the New Deal that had more deeply politicized the country, mobilizing millions with its propaganda and making it clear to many that their very fates depended on what the government could do, or would do. Even when Roosevelt had proclaimed that "Dr. Win the War" had replaced "Dr. New Deal," the public image of a nation in arms had simply taken over many of the same ideals. During the war, the country had still portrayed itself as it had when fighting the Depression: as Uncle Sam with his sleeves rolled up (or as Rosie the Riveter, since for the first time a large number of white women found jobs, as their black counterparts had done long before). The workers in serried ranks had become soldiers, their banners no longer the blue eagle of the NRA but simply the Stars and Stripes. The basic image had remained the same: a nation mobilized, energy summoned; a people united, ready to get the job done.

Subsequently, during the late forties and early fifties, Americans still debated many of the issues that had been raised by the New Deal in the thirties, and they thought about new issues in similar ways, although a number of social aims had been forgotten or at least put away for the duration. During the War, the "job" had been simply: to win. Not much else was demanded of us. The Axis powers were evil, but not too much was said about the details. Accounts of genocide began to appear in the mainstream press as early as 1942, but they were extremely limited, and propaganda ads and posters depicting the Germans never hinted at this in explaining why we fought. Hollywood was even worse—no American film mentioned the Holocaust until well after the war. This was partly because of pressure from leaders of the American Jewish community, who were acutely aware of the country's prevailing anti-Semitism and didn't want to do anything that would lead the general public to feel that the war was being waged on behalf of the Jews. But the Jewish studio heads had also been explicitly warned by Washington to stay off the subject, and they had knuckled under in a cowardly fashion. Nor was there any hint of the massacre of millions of non-Jews in the East by the Germans that had occurred even before the extermination camps had been put in place. Indeed, Hollywood went even further to show the Germans to be, for the most part, much like us, albeit somewhat nastier. Not so with Hollywood's portrayal of the Japanese. A few years ago, when I published John Dower's history of the Pacific War, *War Without Mercy*, Dower organized a showing of films about the war made by Japanese and American filmmakers. The Japanese films were low-key and relatively honest, centered on the tragic necessity imposed on their population. American films, on the other hand, were overtly racist, in the "kill the little yellow monkeys" vein; some gleefully showed soldiers with flamethrowers "cleaning out" Pacific island caves and other hiding places, a Hiroshima in slow motion.

More recently, I went back through all the wartime issues of *Life* magazine that I had collected so religiously as a child. I decided to look particularly at the ads, both to see how much I had remembered and to uncover what they had conveyed to the American reader about our war aims. In a country without an official Ministry of Propaganda, it had been left to the private sector to guide the citizen through the uncertainties of war, as had also been the case in 1917. Though a certain number of the ads showed German and particularly Japanese soldiers to be the kind of people who wouldn't hesitate to mistreat women and children, there wasn't much more in the way of explaining why, precisely, we were fighting. But if you had been able to ask *Life*'s advertisers what the war's challenges were, and they were to answer honestly, they would have admitted that the chore was "maintaining our market share." The ads made obvious that these companies were most concerned with either keeping their name in the public eye by showing how helpful they were in the war effort—*Lucky Strikes have gone to War*—or in commiserating with consumers about the terrible suffering involved in having to go without their product until the final victory. (In reality, I can remember very few shortages in our daily life during the war beyond the difficulty of finding cigarettes for my father, who was reduced to smoking unheard-of brands such as Lady Hamilton. And as soon as France was liberated we had been able to send endless parcels of food, such as Nescafé and jam, which were never lacking in the U.S., to our deprived European family.)

Far more numerous in those old magazines, however, were ads that were quite specific indeed: ads that showed what the wonders of the postwar period would entail. Big-ticket items predominated. People were promised that once the war was won, we would not be facing the old Depression but a new, postwar paradise. Ad after ad invoked a future in which large plate-glass windows and fluorescent lighting transformed our lives, as we finally basked in the glories of the new refrigerators and cars that had been kept from us. America would be the closest thing to heaven since the 1939 World's Fair; the utopian imagination of the ad agencies had not progressed greatly since then.

The government, meanwhile, was less imaginative in what it had to offer. To be sure, in 1942 Roosevelt and Churchill had proclaimed the Atlantic Charter, which in time would lead to the creation of the United Nations. But the Charter seemed a kind of watered-down, international version of Roosevelt's Four Freedoms—freedom of speech and worship, and freedom from want and fear—in the way that it offered a series of vague and encouraging war aims primarily to the colonial world. Like a salesman worried that dissatisfied customers will come back to haunt him, nothing all that specific was said about the kind of Better World that was supposed to be in store. And the Charter was aimed abroad more than at America. All those dusky fellows in Southeast Asia who were being counted on to rescue our downed airmen had to have a little something to look forward to. Many of the postwar revolts can be linked to the excessive trust that the natives did, in fact, place in the Charter's assurances—the Indonesians, for example, pathetically quoting our Declaration of Independence in their new government's first public statements, even as the U.S. stood by to let the Dutch recapture their former and very profitable colony. At Yale, Professor Paul Mus, the French anthropologist, once told me of being sent to Indochina as the war ended to tell Ho Chi Minh that de Gaulle had decided that the French would take over his country from the combination of Vichy and Japanese forces that had run it during the war— in other words, the Axis forces against whom Ho had fought. Mus described Ho waiting for him, in what I imagined was a tent in the jungle, sitting at a small table on which stood a bucket containing a bottle of champagne that Ho had somehow scavenged, planning to toast Indo-Chinese independence. Meanwhile, de Gaulle had already told Japanese forces to maintain their hold on the country until he could replace them with his troops. The French, like the Dutch in Indonesia, the English in Malaya, and the Americans in the Philippines, were moving as quickly as they could to reinstate the status quo ante.

The majority of Americans were largely unaware of all this, and despite the murky outlines of our country's future, they nonetheless felt sure that things would be better. The British wartime films portrayed it most brilliantly, however—usually with a final shot in which the hero, reclining in a hospital bed, would look out the window to see the clouds parting to reveal a new sun, while the narrator would praise the sacrifices of The People's War, as it was then called, and the promise of a brighter future would be pledged anew.

The British, the Europeans in general, were far clearer about what needed to be done. In most of Europe, Socialist victories in the postwar elections were so overwhelming that their programs could be enacted right away. European citizens were assured that theirs would be a secure future, that the sharing of sacrifice that had been imposed during the war would be continued. In England, for example, despite limited rations, many in the working class found themselves eating far healthier meals than before the war. Instead of a diet consisting basically of "bread and drippings," the government assured even babies unheard-of luxuries, such as orange juice, and guaranteed milk for all schoolchildren.

To make sure that wartime equality would be continued, a program of nationalization of key industries, extending the welfare state and a continuation of the Popular Front programs of the thirties, became common throughout Europe. Collaborators and extreme rightists in Europe were purged. Even de Gaulle, hardly a socialist but ruling in coalition with the Left, imposed massive state takeovers. Mining, public utilities, and armaments were all nationalized, so that by 1946 a fifth of French industries were publicly owned. All the newspapers in France were taken over and given to the journalists themselves. (De Gaulle, eager to have media independent of its former and often corrupt owners, created papers like *Le Monde* from the wreckage—and offices—of the old, contaminated newspapers. In Paris in 1948, there were thirty-eight daily newspapers. Because of the acute paper short-age, they were limited at first to two pages per edition, but they gave their readers a choice that had never been thought possible before the war.)

In America, there were no such clear plans. To be sure, things would be better. Justice would be done for the veterans. There would be no return to the Depression, which, after all, had lasted until the war began. Years later, I had a conversation with Leon Keyserling, Truman's chief economic advisor, who described to me how worried the administration had been in the forties that, without the wartime expenditures, the country would again face massive unemployment. The idea that the war and the war alone had rescued the American economy was no Marxist canard. It was accepted as self-evident, and postwar Keynesian legislation assuming full employment as a national priority had widespread support. As Eric Hobsbawm reminds us in *The Age of Extremes,* even as centrist an economist as Paul Samuelson had worried in 1943 that America might experience "the greatest period of unemployment and industrial dislocation which any economy has ever faced."[11] As the war ended, there was some debate as to whether 2 percent unemployment was the goal or whether it could go a little higher. The idea that within the coming years the Democrats would live with double-digit unemployment, much less that urban minorities would suffer 30 percent joblessness, would have been dismissed as ludicrous scaremongering. (The most recent figures for New York, those of 2005, show joblessness among all black and Latino males between ages 16 and 64 at 39.3 percent. That figure

---

[11] Hobsbawm, *The Age of Extremes* (New York: Pantheon Books, 1990), 230.

represents people unlikely ever to find jobs, not just temporarily unemployed.)

In the end, when it came time to define his campaign in 1948, Truman proposed his Fair Deal, a much milder version of Roosevelt's policies. It included some innovative social programs, among them a national health-insurance program, which were never enacted. Critics such as Studs Terkel, a Wallace advocate, argue that Truman launched his modest version of the New Deal merely to capture votes that might have gone to Wallace and the Progressive Party. And certainly, there was considerable room for Truman to move the party to the left, especially with the Dixiecrats luring away racist Southern Democrats and with Republicans so aggressively trying to undo Roosevelt's reforms—a leitmotif of GOP policy to this day.

Mild as Truman's policies may have seemed compared to those being enacted in Europe, my memory of those years is of a world bubbling with political debate and expectation. For the first time in American history, college campuses were becoming hotbeds of activity, thanks in large part to the GI Bill, which allowed all veterans access to a higher education. It suddenly populated colleges with a totally different class (and age) of student. Soon, campuses nationwide were the scenes of animated debates between the differing factions, and there was a general feeling that much needed to be changed. On another front—a barely reported one—there was the presence of returning black veterans, angry at their time in a Jim Crow army, wanting to challenge segregation back home. The number of lynchings soared, and black veterans were roughed up and shot at simply for trying to register to vote.

* * *

I can hardly claim that my grade school was aflame with such controversy. But, incredible as it may seem to parents of school-age
children today, the scholastic newspaper that we were assigned to
read every week—which had the quaint nineteenth-century name
My Weekly Reader and was circulated not merely to progressive
schools but to most public schools across the country—kept us
abreast of current events and the new governmental proposals
that our elders were discussing. As the 1948 elections approached,
its pages were filled with an ever-increasing number of diagrams.
Little boxes proliferated, representing new public housing units
or dams that would be built once we approved the many offspring
of the TVA, the New Deal's hugely successful Tennessee Valley
Authority. (This meant not only more publicly generated electric-
ity; it meant rebuilding impoverished areas and improving not
only their environment but their social infrastructure.) Other
boxes represented the new hospital beds that would be needed if
Truman's proposals for national health insurance were to get
through. The *Reader* was like a Rooseveltian monopoly board on
which the units of progress could be seen accumulating before
our very eyes. Soon the whole country would be covered with
these symbols of prosperity and well-being. It would come as a
shock to the current-day Republicans to realize that schoolchildren were not only offered these visions, but asked to debate
whether the mines and railroads should be nationalized, as had
happened in most of Western Europe.

My own socialist ideas were far from marginalized. They were
assumed to be part of the debate. (During a recent viewing of a

forties-era film version of Thornton Wilder's ultra-sentimental, Pulitzer Prize-winning *Our Town*, I was amused when the narrator described the conservative politics of the typical town but conceded that 4 percent of its inhabitants voted Socialist.)

Not everyone in my Quaker school agreed with the proposals for a Fair Deal. Many of my classmates were staunch Republicans. (The father of a few would even become a member of Eisenhower's future cabinet.) But we all understood that the question before us was not whether the government should be downsized or gradually eliminated; the question was not "Should we?" but rather "How much?" The New Deal, after all, was barely a decade behind us, and its issues were still very present in our minds. My history teacher, a classic New Deal Democrat, had his desk piled high with transcripts of the hearings held by the Temporary National Economic Commission, which had debated Roosevelt's key policies. He never assigned them to us, but their impact on his teaching was obvious. . . as was their symbolism as rapidly aging documents.

But beyond the classroom, the media at the time still discussed the questions of the thirties, and the issues did not seem abstract or unclear. Whether through photos or "artists' conceptions," I had a very clear picture of what our better future would look like: Public housing was invariably pictured from the ground up, focusing on tree-filled playgrounds in which children gamboled, while through the leafy branches one could glimpse the modest but salubrious housing in which Americans were now entitled to live. I grew up feeling that my fellow Americans agreed in general that everyone had a right to decent housing—that part of our postwar posterity would be to help the third of the country that was, as Roosevelt so memorably put it, "ill-housed, ill-clad, ill-nourished." There were no forebodings of the vast, desolate "projects," suitable only for dynamiting, that would eventually be built. In fact, if you wander around Manhattan looking at the older housing projects, it's striking to see how many trees there are, how comfortably low the buildings, how relatively homelike and nonthreatening the sites are. I can recall nobody worrying that the projects of the era were being built only in the poor, mostly black areas. Where else should they have been built? It was not even considered that old patterns of segregation were being reinforced. It was remarkable enough that Truman was working to desegregate the army.

I later realized that I had grown up in a city that seemed to have no blacks at all. When I walked through the part of Manhattan where I lived, there were no Negroes, as we then called them, to be seen except the occasional servant. (In high school one of my classmates, whose father was a vice president of Macy's department store, told us of a discussion launched by her father at the dinner table concerning Macy's' decision to finally hire black salesclerks despite the widespread industry belief that no New Yorker would ever buy from a Negro. Macy's went ahead with the historic change regardless, and none of its customers seemed to notice.)

If there were no black potential muggers in the street, one could still feel fear. As I've mentioned, the threat to me came from the white Irish "Dead-End Kids" who lived a couple of blocks away from posh Park Avenue. But even my experience with the anti-Semitic toughs with whom I went to school did not create an anti-working-class backlash in my mind—that is, a feeling that these people did not deserve decent housing or health care. Those were givens. The idea that I might choose not to support these measures never occurred to me. The right-wing joke now current about a neocon being a liberal who has been mugged would have been incomprehensible to me. There were certain things a just society demanded, an ethical imperative which everyone agreed upon, no matter their religion or creed.

* * *

Politics to me became the way to apply these ethical demands to our society. The theologian Reinhold Niebuhr said that he was a Socialist not because he denied original sin, but precisely because he believed in it. Though not everyone agreed with him, the religious basis of socialism was a very strong one. Whether one followed R. H. Tawney's Christian Socialism or some variant of it, there were many clerics of all faiths that found an argument for social justice, at the very least, in their tradition. One of the first serious paperbacks I ever bought was *The Christian Demand for Social Justice*, by Bishop William Scarlett. His ideas were accessible enough for the book to be distributed in cigar stores and drugstores throughout the country. I remember paying thirty-five cents for it.

Like all good reformers, I was not swayed by the ideas of class war or armed revolution. My innate social-democratic conservatism was compounded by the anti-Communist hysteria surrounding us, which prevented anything coming from the far Left from having any credibility. Much to my horror, when the fare for the New York subway system was raised from five to ten cents, the American Labor Party issued a statement saying that if the

Democrats could be responsible for such perfidy, a further raise to fifteen cents might be next. I refused to believe such dire predictions, because of my optimistic faith in a fair America, but also because I knew that the ALP and its leader, Congressman Vito Marcantonio, were reputed to be backed by the Reds and therefore not to be believed.

Totally oblivious of my failure to listen to others, I believed that my own Socialist credo was so obviously convincing that it was simply a question of explaining the Socialist position to enough people. I suppose that I had imbibed Descartes with my mother's milk: I believed people were rational and that, in time, the logic of Socialist arguments would persuade them. Since I'd been in the sixth grade, Social Democracy had seemed to me the only policy that would bring about true equality and justice.

Little did any of us Socialists—and I can probably include Norman Thomas, for whom I rooted in 1948—realize that far from seizing the commanding heights of the economy, as we had done in Europe, Socialists and their policies were subsidizing the crumbling infrastructure of capitalism. While many of Europe's nationalized companies, such as Renault and Volkswagen, worked extremely well, many others were in bad shape when they were taken over. For example, there was very little that the British Labour government could do to maintain the mines and steel mills they had taken over so happily, once they had begun to realize how technologically behind these were, how vulnerable to overseas competition.

Nor did capitalists of the time realize that the Socialist reforms underway in Europe would help them in the long run. They feared that nationalization programs—such as that of the railroads, for example—would be more than the rescue of hopelessly unprofitable but essential services; they feared these programs would lead to greater state control.

In any event, the issue of public ownership was a central one, and one that I followed closely and passionately. Very few of my classmates agreed with me, though none seemed shocked at the positions I took. I often found myself in long debates in the school cafeteria with other children, some much to my left. In addition to the Republicans I mentioned, another of my classmates was a devout Trotskyite, the son of a distinguished New York intellectual. Another was one of the few adherents of the Progressive Party in our school. It never occurred to me at the time to wonder whether other school cafeterias throughout the country contained similar distributions of opinion. I assumed as a matter of course that there were little Trotskyites and little Social Democrats arguing the same questions from coast to coast. In recent years, discussing this period with others, I've been relieved to find friends with similar memories; for instance, the historian Gabriel Kolko told me that he recalled having similar discussions with his classmates in Akron, Ohio.

Likewise, when I attended election meetings and rallies in New York, I didn't feel that I was the only thirteen-year-old interested. I once stood in a very heterogeneous crowd in Union Square to see Harry Truman (finding myself surprised, after knowing him only through black-and-white newspaper photos, to see him in living color). Lining up outside Madison Square Garden to hear Tom Dewey along with thousands of Republicans, I was assured by neighbors that theirs was a better class of people, but not necessarily an older one.

Clearly my situation was not a typical one; the world of *Grease* and other such films nostalgic for the fifties was completely alien to me. Yet it would be wrong to consider my experience unique. I remain all the more impressed by how I reflected opinions that were widely held by those interested in politics, then still a large part of the population.

I wasn't the only one who knew that Henry Wallace was a fellow traveler and that his Progressive Party was probably run by the Communists, although it was only much later that I read Dwight MacDonald's devastating critiques. Wallace had been an impressive secretary of agriculture under Roosevelt and had been responsible for many of the most imaginative and daring reforms in the New Deal—assuring the opposition of the mainstream party. He could have been Roosevelt's running mate in 1944, but the party machine did everything in its power to nominate the far more conservative Truman instead. Well before the campaign of '48, I knew that the Communists were no longer a good thing; that much as we had liked them during the war, those halcyon popular-front days were well behind us. Years later, teaching a Yale seminar on postwar public opinion, I went through the political and literary magazines of the day and was struck by how early the anticommunist campaigns had begun. After the war, the Right had held its fire for only a very short time. By 1947, with the publication of *I Chose Freedom* by Victor Kravchenko, the battle had been carried home. Kravchenko had defected from the Soviet embassy in Canada, and his book was used to make sure that Stalin's crimes would be pinned on his allies in America. It sold millions of copies. Reading the book again recently, I was struck by how careful its last chapters were in incriminating a large number of American leftists, such as Wallace and even Wendell Willkie, the 1944 Republican presidential candidate and one-worlder— people I suspect Kravchenko had never met or read. It seemed to me far more likely that the FBI had supplied names, and had perhaps even ghostwritten an important part of the book. But while there was a great deal of debate about the evils of Communism, the political atmosphere of the late forties had not yet been poisoned by the fears of the McCarthy era. Liberals and Truman Democrats were increasingly anti-Communist, both in reaction to the Russian betrayals of our naïve hopes for an independent Eastern Europe but also in support of Truman's aggressive Cold War policies. Truman had already purged every possible Communist sympathizer from his administration. In theory, McCarthy had nothing to object to in what the Democrats had done.

In spite of my French background, I was totally ignorant of the strong European opposition to the Cold War, to the Continent's growing neutralism and the feeling that Europe's democracies had to stand away from the growing clash of the two superpowers. *Le Monde* and other influential papers took a strong neutralist line, arguing that there was no need for Europe to be caught up in this great power conflict. It was only much later, when I studied in England, that I became aware of these currents, of the attempts in the early fifties to create a neutralized Central Europe, in the way that Austria had been neutral after the war. The Gaitskell-Rapacki plan, formed by the British Labour leader Hugh Gaitskell and the Polish foreign minister Adam Rapacki, would have created a weapon-free neutral zone in Central Europe rather than a rearmed Germany linked to NATO. But these proposals came a few years later, as Europe's neutralism became more evidently concrete. As far as I was concerned, the Cold War was a clearly defined battle between good and evil.

I had read *The God that Failed*, the anthology of commentaries on Communism that included a chapter by Gide, as soon as it was published. I felt on very familiar ground. I had grown up in an atmosphere that was solidly anti-Stalinist, though we rarely talked about politics at home. My mother jokingly described herself as a Jacobin. My father, like most French intellectuals, was clearly on the Left, but I rarely heard in any greater detail about exactly where he stood. I did know that he had been born in Baku, in Czarist Russia, to a father who had become very wealthy in the oil business at a time when fortunes were being created from the Crimean oil rush. Appropriately, given their wealth, the family were centrist Constitutional Democrats, not Socialists. No doubt this family influence, this heritage of the thirties, led to my being a premature—indeed *immature*—anti-Communist. But so strong were the currents in America at the time that I would doubtless have been swept into the liberal branch of anti-Communism that would prevail for years to come.

* * *

After Truman's victory, a strong right-wing counterattack was launched. In spite of Truman's having purged the Communists from his administration and launched some aggressive Cold War policies, a different battle was about to begin. Much has been made of McCarthy's surprise at the attention given to his now-famous speech in Wheeling, West Virginia, where he waved a list of what he claimed were "known Communists" still in the government. The list had been pasted together at the last minute, an inaccurate potpourri of old accusations pieced together from the files of the FBI and the Republican National Committee. Leon Keyserling, Truman's economic adviser, was one of the few people at the time to ask himself who, exactly, had put this list together, and with what intentions. But these were private doubts, mentioned to me years later. The press did not dare ask such questions. The result is that even today there are those surprised to learn that McCarthy failed to uncover even one Communist in the State Department.

It still amazes me that after all these years there are still people who believe that McCarthy was in fact only attacking Communists, and that the names of non-Communists that constantly showed up in his lists or inquiries were the result of sloppy research or drunken mis-filings. It seems clear to me that the names were carefully chosen to indicate the kind of New Deal civil servant whom the Right wanted to purge, now that Truman had actually already eliminated the Communists. Suddenly the names of respected liberals and social democrats began to appear, people such as Wolf Ladejinsky, the head of land reform in Japan under MacArthur and the architect of a policy that was to mark the success of the American occupation; and Val Lorwin, an expert in labor relations working for the American Embassy in Paris. Both were not only impeccable civil servants, they were staunch anti-Communists. By adding them to his list, McCarthy moved politics into a new arena. Whether this was a brilliant stroke on his part or whether he simply accepted any name that was given him, we may never know. But now liberals and old New

Dealers were on the defensive: They had to prove that they were as anti-Communist as any Republican. The Right would define the limits of loyalty and of debate. The Left fell headlong into this carefully laid trap.

Even moderate Republicans were all too pleased to jump on this shaky bandwagon. Eisenhower famously failed to defend his old comrade, General George C. Marshall, when McCarthy included Marshall on a list of traitors. Eisenhower's own speeches, too, increasingly accepted the lie that America had been thoroughly subverted by the Reds. The Republicans would use this theme viciously against Truman and in the ensuing elections, insisting that it was treason within the Democratic administrations that had "lost" first Eastern Europe and then China.

At the very moment that should have been the liberals' triumph—Truman's unexpected victory—the Democrats found themselves on the defensive. No matter how tough their foreign policy, they had to show that they were in no way pro-Communist. What better way than to gradually abandon parts of the Fair Deal, modest as it was? Hopes for a national health-insurance plan were abandoned, as were Truman's attempts at dealing with political bias in the media. (A long-forgotten report, called *A Free and Responsible Press*, was published by his commission on the press, and it raised issues of independence and fairness in corporate-controlled newspapers.) America diverged farther and farther from the postwar Welfare states of Europe, and the division continues to this day. Thus, the Cold War had the result not only of changing our domestic agenda, but of making America increasingly distant from Europe's Socialists and other reformers. Whereas the New Deal had let us maintain close ties with Europe's reformers, we were now becoming irreparably alienated from them.

Truman was made to feel that the need now was for ever-greater internal repression, the proponents of which struck out at Communists past and present with increasing vindictiveness. It was no longer a question of Communists in government; it became a question of Communist war veterans buried in military cemeteries, of Communist pensioners on Social Security, or of Communist teachers in the grade schools. The mystery writer Dashiell Hammett was summoned before the House Un-American Activities Committee to testify on the ridiculous charge that he might have taken royalty money earned through the sale of his books to government libraries and spent it on Communist causes. It was typical of the kind of ludicrous stretch regularly employed by McCarthy in order to browbeat well-known Americans. (Hammett subsequently went to jail when he refused to name his former associates.) As McCarthyism progressed, the purges became ever more punitive and petty, with the goal of punishing people for ever having been involved in a cause that the Communists might have backed. Studs Terkel, with whom I worked for decades, was never a Communist, but he was a happy signer of every petition put before him. ("I never met a petition I didn't like" he explains.) Thanks to that, he lost all his very successful jobs in broadcasting, including his TV show, *Studs' Place*, one of the most popular programs in the early days of television. Overnight he became an unperson. When he finally got a job as a disc jockey on a small FM station, the Chicago *Tribune* would not even include his show in its listings. All this was more than punishment. It was prophylactic: Surely those who saw what was happening would think twice before giving money or joining a demonstration.

* * *

I am surprised when I read descriptions of the fifties that suggest that people weren't all that afraid, that things weren't as bad as they've been made out to be. Of course, there was no Gestapo or KGB, no concentration camp around the corner. But for many the possibility of losing a job or a pension, particularly in their later years, was terrifying enough.

It is hard to document the spread of fear. There have been all too few oral histories or PhD theses on the lesser-known victims. Going back through the papers and magazines of the period, one can clearly see the change of tone, the purge of contributors, starting from about 1950, but the process was gradual and in some ways subtle. One American historian of the period has calculated, for instance, that no one who had written on China for the *New York Times Book Review* before 1950 ever did so again. I noticed the change in which books were deemed worthy of review and in those "credentialized" to write about them. The *NYTBR*, which in the immediate postwar period had placed on its front page an enthusiastic review by Arthur Schlesinger, Jr. of the Beveridge report, the key document of the British welfare state, after 1950 ran only far more conservative articles by Schlesinger. Articles by Russian-army defectors and others considered more knowledgeable than American academics or journalists began to appear regularly. Within a few years, the tone of the *NYTBR* had been completely altered, as had that of nearly all other publications.

Even I, staunch anti-Communist that I was, soon realized the change of atmosphere. I know that during the 1948 campaign, when I visited the Wallace headquarters, it never occurred to me to worry, to fear that someone might look askance at the materials I brought back to school (though a friend who grew up in a Communist family remembers that by 1948 he took home his copy of the progressive New York daily, *PM*, carefully concealed in another paper), but by the early fifties, when I went to what was probably the last of the city's Communist bookstores, the Jefferson School Bookstore off Union Square near my school, the store's clerks considerately nodded in a warning fashion to the overhead cameras, letting me know that the FBI was watching. A show of bravado, a wave and a grin at the hidden observer, was practically mandatory for a self-respecting teenager. The people in the store were worried on my behalf; they no longer expected stray customers to come in off the street. I took home the store's pamphlets, including an early edition of Mao's *On Peoples' Democratic Rule.* I read them and kept them on my bookshelf. I cringe to admit it, but I feel it would be withholding important evidence not to confess: I neatly labeled each pamphlet *Communist Propaganda,* in anticipation of the FBI's eventual perusal of my library.

Teenage paranoia? The remnants of refugee anxiety? One might well think so. An event about that time, 1949 to be exact, suggests otherwise: I had invited my classmates to our apartment to a belated fourteenth birthday party; it would be a "Communist party," and I told them they should dress accordingly. I had prepared an appropriate series of games and all went well until, halfway through the afternoon, someone knocked on the door and I found myself facing a total stranger, a handsome, neatly dressed young man who said he was from the FBI. I must have seen enough movies to be subconsciously prepared for this moment: I asked for identification, and the stranger flashed a plastic portfolio of cards that I could barely make out. He asked a few questions and then left the room, ostensibly to talk to my parents. After a few minutes of agonized discussion with my classmates, I decided to seek him out. I found him in our living room, having a drink with my parents and sharing their laughter at my father's practical joke.

In retrospect, what strikes me about this incident is that not a single one of my classmates, all children of upper-middle-class professionals, many of them loyal Republicans, doubted for a minute that their mail had been opened, the invitation discovered, and the FBI called in. I'm sure we all felt that we could give a satisfactory explanation and be let off with a light warning, but the point is that we had all learned to accept and internalize the lessons of McCarthy. Some of my friends' parents were, in fact, visited by FBI agents and asked to peruse vast photo albums of suspected Communists. Well-dressed young men came to ask questions of my father, too, although some of them may have been from the OSS, whose voluminous files on the refugee population can now be examined by researchers in Washington. I remember going with my father to the home of his old friend Boris Souvarine, who, in the 1920s, had been one of the very first French Communists to denounce Stalin, and who had continued his campaign against the Party into the 1950s. His living room had huge card indexes filled with information that I assume he shared with both the OSS and the FBI. (To be sure, Souvarine was a happy and willing collaborator, fearing the resurgence of Communist influence in France. He thought this could occur partly through the complicity of de Gaulle, who had sought Soviet backing to offset the reluctance of Roosevelt and Churchill to recognize his government.)[12]

The FBI had other, less direct ways of entering our lives and our minds. I used to listen each Sunday to the staccato broadcasts of Walter Winchell, then one of the most popular—and powerful—radio broadcasters. It would later be revealed that the FBI director J. Edgar Hoover fed Winchell a steady diet of information and innuendo, which he duly broadcast.

·   Fear can also be documented by what is not done: It is striking how little information was provided, or reported, that might have inspired opposition to our fighting a devastating war in Korea, especially so soon after the end of the Second World War. Most Americans agreed on the need to fight, seeing it as the start of the much-expected "hot war" between Cold War superpowers. Only a handful of people, like the journalists I. F. Stone and his British counterpart James Cameron, criticized the war in Korea. They were seen as Communist apologists. Cameron was actually dismissed from the Beaverbrook press for his courageous coverage of a war that ravaged the entire Korean peninsula and killed millions of Koreans. Bruce Cumings' history of North Korea quotes reports that at least eighteen of the twenty-two major cities were virtually obliterated, not to mention countless villages of no military or industrial significance. Though the war was called a limited one,

---

[12] Indeed, Eisenhower was so suspicious of de Gaulle that he had originally planned to rule liberated France through an American military government, as he would Germany, and had gone so far as to have an American currency printed for use in France.

our bombing strategy, well before China's intervention, resembled the air war against Japan, and more napalm was dropped on the hapless Koreans than we were to use during the whole of the Vietnam War. But none of this could be learned by reading our papers.

The absence of Korea in the intellectual life of the times is also noteworthy. The *Partisan Review* issued a special edition devoted to American politics in 1952 without ever mentioning the Korean War. Even more recently, it has been absent from memoirs of the period. Dan Wakefield's 1992 book *New York in the 50s* follows his own life and that of a dozen noted journalists and authors in great detail, and the war never appears as a factor in their lives. In 350 pages, there are all of four mentions of the war, centering on the risk of the draft. Nothing is said of the millions killed or the obliterated peninsula.

Had I been reading I. F. Stone's reporting, I would have learned much that might well have changed my mind. But my internal censors were well in place, and I, too, dismissed him as a Communist apologist. I had decided not to read the few daily left-wing newspapers that New York offered, which seemed too pro-Communist to my Cold War eyes. First *PM*, then the *Compass*, then the *Star*, all of which went out of business, one succeeding the last in those tricky years. All had run Stone's articles, but by 1952, they had all disappeared. Nor could Stone find a publisher for his books. Every American and British firm he tried refused, and it was finally the newly born Monthly Review Press that came out with Stone's *The Truman Era* in 1953. At the same time, he decided to launch his own newsletter, at $5 per year, for which he was able to get five thousand brave subscribers, all of whom must have assumed that their act would be noted by the FBI. After the death of his beloved Roosevelt, Stone was unrelenting in his attacks on Truman. Some of his comments have a strange resonance as I write this in 2006: "Mr. Truman's fears transmitted themselves to those around him and through him, to the country, as Mr. Roosevelt's courage had done earlier. 'Toughness' became a mask for weakness, and stubbornness a substitute for strength. Mr. Truman, who was really scared, launched the 'get tough' policy. Mr. Roosevelt, who was really tough, did not need to proclaim that fact to the world."[13]

Very few people had read Stone on the Korean war when his articles appeared in those ever-dwindling opposition papers. I can recall no public protests about the war, nor demonstrations, nor even qualms expressed in private. Not even in our Quaker school, where one might have expected some opposition to the war simply because it was a war. On the contrary, our school and all the other schools in New York were closed so that we could join the crowds viewing the ticker-tape parade to celebrate General Douglas MacArthur's return after he was dismissed by Truman. At least the madmen who seem to be present in most administrations were kept in check, rather than encouraged to run the whole show, as has happened under George W. Bush. We did not know at the time that MacArthur had proposed dropping fifty atomic bombs along the thirty-eighth parallel dividing the two countries, to make sure that a radioactive border would keep Korea forever divided. But we did know that he had gone well beyond his man-

---

[13] Stone, *The Truman Era, 1945-1952* (New York: Monthly Review Press, 1953), xxii.

date of defending the South in invading the North, despite warnings that this would bring China into the war.

Still, and for decades afterward, with the rare exception of historians such as Bruce Cumings, few questioned our government's actions or motives in Korea. Perhaps because I had been in France the previous year, where the opposition to the war was widespread, I felt that there was not enough in the press to answer all my questions. Like others in 1950, I accepted the action in Korea as a necessity, but I wanted to find out more about its causes. Not trusting the Communists, and still, regrettably, suspicious of I. F. Stone, I decided to go to the United Nations headquarters in midtown Manhattan to read their reports on the war's origins. The U.N. librarian produced them without any question, though he must have been surprised at seeing his youthful visitor. I can still recall my uncomfortable discovery that things were not at all as clear-cut as I had been told. There was, in fact, much to be criticized in both halves of Korea, including a long history of border skirmishes and broken promises by the South's Rhee government. (In the end, my discoveries were not enough to persuade me to abandon my support of American policies; I'd learned early on that loyal Social Democrats were not always allowed the luxury of a clear champion. As had happened during the First World War, we would have to compromise occasionally to go along with our government.)

But the number of leftist journals continued to diminish, making it hard to find dissenting opinions on more than just Korea. When I discovered that the headquarters for the Socialist Party were near my school, I began to make occasional pilgrimages to the vast, dark, and nearly empty loft on Fourth Avenue and Twenty-third Street to buy a copy of their pathetic four-page newspaper, *The Socialist Call.* I would give the editor a condescending chuckle as I told him how much I enjoyed reading his accounts of Milwaukee's Socialist mayor, or the activities of the Allentown, Pennsylvania, branch. But even I realized I was driven more by nostalgia than by reality. The days when Manhattan's Lower East Side could elect a Socialist to represent it in Congress, such as when it elected Meyer London, or when Eugene V. Debs could run for president of the United States from his prison cell, were well behind us. The once-influential immigrant Socialist groups had been successfully integrated into the New Deal Democrats. Many of their unions had merged into the more conservative American Federation of Labor. The few remaining Socialists had no illusions, and by the 1952 elections, when they ran a worthy gentleman called Darlington Hoopes for president, they invented a campaign song whose only words were, *"We're voting for Darlington Hoopes / Tra la, Hoopes, tra la, Hoopes, tra la."*

* * *

I realized that there was more to Socialism than this American phantom. After all, Socialists were in power in many other countries, particularly in Western Europe. However, their achievements were barely covered in American newspapers. So, I set about becoming better informed about what Socialists were accomplishing overseas. Fortuitously, a family friend gave me a subscription to the weekly version of the *Manchester Guardian*, and its flimsy onionskin pages brought me much of the news I so craved. I also read as many other foreign newspapers and magazines as I could get hold of, such as *Le Monde* and, particularly, the *New Statesman,* in which I enviously pored over the small ads announcing all the meetings and discussions going on in London.

In order to get such hard-to-find publications, as well as what remained of the American leftist press, I began to frequent what seemed the only newsstand left in New York where such papers were available—a well-stocked kiosk on Forty-second Street, just down from the New York Public Library. Its owner was a red-faced older man wearing terribly thick glasses. Rather than sell the glossies and pinup magazines featured by his competitors, he sold the few remaining Communist papers, British weeklies such as the *Tribune,* the Bevanite left-wing Labour paper, and the first issues of *Dissent,* with its jagged and deliberately shocking masthead. It was reassuring to me; it meant that I must not be the country's only remaining dissenter, as there had to have been a sufficient number of us amongst New York's millions to warrant such a lavish display of dissidence. (Years later, when I was an editor, I went back to visit this unsung hero of the McCarthy period to thank him for what he had done. He told me he had hopes of starting a small bookstore, so I sent one of Random House's New York salesmen to visit him. But the salesman came back and shook his head sadly, doubtless convinced that I was an even more hopeless case than he had previously assumed.)

There was one other source of dissent, albeit an unlikely one, a few blocks from my house: a small, progressive Catholic bookshop called The Paraclete. There, near the door, one could always find a pile of Dorothy Day's newspaper, the *Catholic Worker,* selling for a theoretical penny. It looked much more like a religious tract than a newspaper, with its dated woodblock illustrations on the front page, but it made strong egalitarian and pacifist arguments opposing the Korean War. Though I could see myself, an atheist, working with the Friends Service Committee, joining the Catholic Workers never seemed a possible course for me. But it led to a lifelong respect for the Catholic Left, even though this movement diminished over the years as much as that of its secular comrades.

In the end, though, what proved to be the most significant source of subversive information for me hardly gave out such a reassuring vibe: It was a red-brick Victorian building, located a few blocks from Friends Seminary off Union Square, which housed the Rand School. This was the last of the old Socialist Party fronts, an adult education center for workers that was kept going by the loyal help of the ILGWU—the International Ladies Garment Workers Union—and others. For the most part, it offered a standard diet of classes—Italian-language lessons for the children of Italian garment workers who now regretted having never learned their parents' tongue, for example. But lecture courses were offered, occasionally, and somehow, in 1952, Hannah Arendt was hired to teach a class outlining her theory on totalitarianism, based on her monumental book *The Origins of Totalitarianism*, which had just been published. Arendt had worked a series of odd jobs since she had escaped Europe for the U.S. in 1941, including that of editor at Schocken Books. But no one had offered her a proper academic post, and it would be years before the University of Chicago would add her to its faculty. In the meantime, she was teaching a class to five garment workers, my mother, and me.

The setting could not have been more barren: a small, dimly lit room with a few uncomfortable wooden chairs. Nonetheless, Arendt taught us as if she was at Harvard, speaking with passion and precision and without the slightest hint of embarrassment or condescension. It remains to this day one of my most exciting intellectual experiences, far more fulfilling than the classes I would soon thereafter attend at Yale. One of the main themes of Arendt's book and lectures had a special resonance for us: that Hitler was colonizing Europe just as Europe had colonized Africa in the previous century. This must have been a revelation to other exiles in New York as well. Claude Lévi-Strauss, when part of the French faculty at the New School for Social Research, was thinking along similar lines. In an unpublished memo to Jacques Maritain about the role of intellectuals in the Resistance, he argued that it was essential to understand that "In Western Europe, Germany has realized the colonial dream, whose model had previously been constructed on a broader scale." The Resistance, he continued, needed to integrate into its program its opposition to France's rights in "what it calls its empire."[14] This was in total opposition to de Gaulle's insistence on reconquering France's overseas holdings, and it explains in part Lévi-Strauss' opposition to de Gaulle. We can also see here how some of the exiles rallied behind the changes implied by the Atlantic Charter, albeit with a far stronger and more extensive intellectual and political case. In my own mind, the need for colonial liberation merged with the need for freedom in Europe. It became part of my Socialist

---

[14] Quoted in Loyer, *Paris à New York*, 421.

assumptions, which unfortunately would not be shared by all the European Social Democrats—or even by Communists, as during the Algerian war, when the French Communist Party often played the nationalist card.

In addition to the unparalleled excitement of the class with Hannah Arendt, the Rand School had another appeal, although a less expected and less exciting one: In the school office, behind an old-fashioned wooden barrier, was a meager display of pamphlets. They would become my political lifeline for the coming years. The dull covers and uninviting titles were, to me, like a display in a candy-shop window. I had to decide whether I could afford both the Fabian Society pamphlet on workers' control as well as the Labour Party's report on the first years of the nationalized industries. Here, at last, I could discover how "we" were doing since the heady day in 1945 when the victorious Labour MPs had clasped hands in the lobby of Parliament and sung Blake's hymn about turning England into the green and promised land of a new Jerusalem. Whatever our stalemates at home, we could see that governments abroad could take over vast industries and make them work, that a socialized health service was possible.[15] The reports confirmed that we were right, that what I had been arguing about in the school cafeteria was indeed possible, that whatever the

---

[15] Even on our own continent, the Canadian Socialists, then called by the quaint name of the Cooperative Commonwealth Federation, could nationalize the resources of one province, Saskatchewan, and stand up to the pressures of the American oil industry. The state would use its resources to institute a comprehensive health system that would benefit all of its citizens. Workers could be given control of the factories in which they worked; at least, that had been done with a paper factory in Moosejaw, Saskatchewan. The details were burned into my memory, and they were later described at length in an inspiring book by Seymour Lipset, *Agrarian Socialism.*

American press and politicians might be saying, Socialism still represented a real alternative. There was more to life than Eisenhower's Big-Business alliance; more than the oft-repeated quote that what was good for General Motors was good for America.

To learn more, I would visit the British government's information office, high up in Rockefeller Center. There I could read more reports and the British newspapers. I suspect that it was not so much the reading as the actual contact with a government I could believe in that mattered to me. New Jerusalem it might not yet be, but at least here were people who actually believed in the place and were seeking to bring it about. Looking back, I can understand the need of so many Communists to believe that Russia was accomplishing all they had hoped for, and the need of Zionists who had similar hopes for Israel. It helped one to keep the faith. Otherwise, it would have been too easy to be pushed under by the silence and the fear.

By the early fifties, not only had most signs of Communist activity and dissent been successfully erased from the public scene, but even their archenemies, the Socialists and many of the liberals, had been pulled down with them. A cartoon at the time showed a cop with a raised billy club charging a crowd of demonstrators. "But officer, I'm an anti-Communist," a hapless demonstrator protests. To which the cop replies, "I don't care what kind of Communist you are."

* * *

By 1953, when I went to college, we were at the crest of what the press dubbed "the silent generation," although "silenced" would have been a better term. In addition to the political changes, there was the draft and a compulsory Army physical exam as soon as you graduated from high school. I remember the scrawny kids surrounding me as we were examined in my old public school, as the doctors routinely stamped *peds planus*—flat feet—on our form. Peeking at the papers, I was struck by the number of people my age who were also immigrants. Those not college-bound had to face Korea, although at the time this did not seem so terrifying. The coverage of the war had kept it at a distance, far from our living rooms; unlike during Vietnam, there were no awful television images every night. The war did not seem an actual threat to us, nor something that one could and must oppose.

Even at the Friends Seminary, although Quakers had spoken up elsewhere, the ideas of draft resistance and conscientious objection were never mentioned. Nor were we involved in the protests against the civil-defense drills that Tom Dewey, as governor, had imposed on us all: Each week, sirens would remind us of the imminence of atomic attack. Ludicrous shelters were designated throughout the city in buildings that would doubtless have been incinerated had an attack actually occurred. (Only recently was the yellow-and-black sign removed from the lobby of my family's Upper West Side building—just in time for 9/11.) I was so committed to being a good citizen that each week I attended a civil-defense course held in the auditorium of the local Salvation Army mission, whose banners appropriately proclaimed blood and fire—though how much blood and fire was something that we would understand only later. Good Social Democrat that I was, I divided my free time between the Friends Service Committee's relief efforts for the victims of the last war and the preparations for the next one.

While these global threats created an unavoidably tense climate, they did not influence our every minute. There was fear, political fear, that lasted well after McCarthy himself was finally toppled by the Army-McCarthy hearings of 1954. But there was more to our conformity than just politics. I remember an evening spent with the parents of one of my classmates, people who had been teenagers during the Roaring Twenties. They sweetly but seriously tried to discover why we were so very dull, so cautious; why we were so unwilling to take risks, so reluctant to have fun. Certainly our sexuality could not have been more constrained—we used to joke that our favorite sex manual, Eustace Chesser's *Love Without Fear*, should have been called *Fear Without Love*.

Fear, in fact, played a constant role in the relations between the sexes in those pre-Pill days. Even years later at Yale, fewer than one-fifth of my classmates had abandoned their virginity, according to the school's own published surveys. My neighbors in my last years at school were a group of five engineering students, friendly and innocent guys. One of them stayed out very late on a date and his roommates all stayed up to hear from him upon his return. "I was hoping," one of them told me, "that we had become a typical Yale room."

I had literally never heard of drugs. In our high school, even smoking a simple cigarette did not seem quite appropriate, though some of the faster kids did indulge. But even beyond my sedate Quaker School, the general tone was one of caution and conformity. On the other hand, the open political atmosphere that characterized our school debates proved to be far ahead of the rest of the country's mood, as I was to discover upon going to Yale.

When I had come back from France in 1949 to what I thought would be a normal life in New York, I did indeed live a carefree and happy existence for the following year or so, absorbed by politics and life at school. I took as a given that my father's health was not perfect, but I wasn't aware of the gravity of his illnesses: In addition to emphysema, he had contracted lung cancer. He had smoked heavily all his life, so this might have been expected, although we were to learn of it only after his autopsy. Still, I should have guessed that he was gravely ill. He had increasing difficulty going down to Pantheon every day; negotiating the steps at the subway station became harder and harder for him. The last photos show him looking incredibly thin, very much like the concentration-camp survivors we had seen in photographs. But I was used to his appearance, and both he and my mother had succeeded in keeping from me the true state of his health. My father, I think, had persuaded himself that he was in less danger than he was, and that had affected my thinking as well. His death, then, came as a great shock. I had just turned fifteen. Simone, who had spent my father's last years caring for him, was deeply affected. She stopped working, could hardly sleep, felt that her world had ended. . . as indeed it had.

Both of our lives were transformed by my father's death. It took months for my mother to return to something resembling a normal life. Eventually, she was able to find a job as a designer for Mark Cross, the leather-goods maker, and for a while she went to work every day. But it did little to fill the huge gap in her life.

I, meanwhile, was committed to continuing my pleasant teenager's life, but at the same time I felt strongly that somehow

I had to take on a more supportive role—I needed to find work after school, do what I could to help the nonexistent family finances. So, I took on summer jobs on Wall Street, working at the Louis Dreyfus grain-exporting firm run by my father's friends. Once the school year ended, I would show up every day at the enormous red stone building on Battery Park that housed the Produce Exchange. The exchange floor was as vast as Grand Central Station, with three-story-high windows that were always open. A constant stream of pigeons flew over the traders, who were dealing in millions of tons of their future bird feed. Later, I started working after school and weekends at the Eighth Street Bookstore, earning the minimum wage of fifty cents per hour (actually more than it is now, in constant dollars) and coming in sleepily to school the next day. Being the store's youngest employee, I swept the floors and opened the packages of books. But I also learned the titles of all the books in stock and enjoyed what would turn out to be a practical introduction to publishing. Across the street was another bookstore, part of the Womrath chain, which catered to a middlebrow audience and had a rental library full of the current popular fiction. In those days, there were 350 bookstores in New York City, ten times the number there are today. The Eighth Street Bookstore store was small and narrow, but it had nearly all the books that an intellectual New Yorker might want, and it had an impressive clientele, too—although when W. H. Auden came, it was only to ask for the latest mysteries. Still, it was an exiting work for me, much better than my duties on the floor of the Produce Exchange. Some of the clerks next to me at the cash register were said to be Communist cadres, who had been driven underground, though how they could be "underground" while in full view of much of the New York intelligentsia I never figured out.

The few dollars a week that I was able to contribute to our treasury didn't make much difference to my mother, I'm afraid, but they mattered a lot to me in terms of feeling that I was beginning to be a breadwinner, somehow replacing my father, no matter how modestly. Despite my efforts, however, we lived well under the poverty line; while going over old income tax returns recently, I saw that there were years when our income was in the hundreds rather than the thousands. My father had never earned more than a hundred dollars a week at Pantheon—nor had his partners—and toward the end of his life his medicines were costing much more than that. I understood that certain things would be impossible for us—for example, it never occurred to me to learn how to drive, since I assumed that we would never be able to afford a car. (I still don't know how.) In short, we lived very modestly.

But I never thought of us as underprivileged or belonging to the lower class. When I was still a child, Simone had explained the French social system to me: The poor, of course, were at the bottom, then the various layers of the bourgeoisie. But on top of them all were the intellectuals. That was us, and therefore there was never any question of our feeling underprivileged. This rationale had clearly helped Simone to support her new poverty, and it was something I never thought to question.

New York at that time was an easier place to live with little money, and I got to know the city fairly well—or at least, what I thought of as the city. I never went above Ninety-sixth Street, other than to take a bus to the Cloisters, with one exception:

Curiosity about Harlem once led me to walk through its streets, to see what the shops were selling, what differences I could discover. But all I found was poverty and scarcity, no exotic black stores opening up another world. I never ventured back. Nor did I go to the West Side, where I now live, except to make occasional forays to the Thalia, then the city's prime art cinema. Occasionally I would spend the few dollars that allowed me to stand in the highest balcony of the old Metropolitan Opera, on Broadway and Thirty-ninth. My fellow standees were mainly old, shabbily dressed Italian immigrants who seemed to feel very much at home in that lofty space.

I spent much of my time at the Museum of Modern Art, making it my club, having coffee in its lovely, small, gravel-strewn garden, in which there were never more than a handful of people. I also went to see a great many of the classic films shown there, getting another form of education otherwise impossible in those pretelevision days. Kids could get in for a pittance, a quarter I think, and I could go at least once a week. I got to know all of the museum's paintings and was eventually able to distinguish the styles of all the artists. Again, without thinking of it, I was immersing myself deeply in European culture.

Far from feeling myself to be one of the "needy," I felt strong moral pressure to help those who were. Though the war was over, and French children no longer got American vitamins, there were many others in need. As soon as the United Nations Children's Fund (UNICEF) was started, I volunteered to help. I organized a school drive and went down Lexington Avenue for many blocks, badgering every shopkeeper for a donation. This was well before UNICEF became famous and arranged such drives throughout the country, and many a would-be donor looked at me suspiciously. But my classmates and I managed to raise a thousand dollars, and I like to think that, seeing what we had done, the UN decided that they might encourage others to do the same. The theory of survivor guilt had not yet been invented, but even if I had been presented with it, I am sure I would have argued that what I was doing was the only correct way to behave, that being a refugee had nothing to do with it.

Later, I felt that I should not simply raise money but help through my own physical efforts. I had heard that the Friends meeting house on Gramercy Park needed help preparing relief supplies for Europe. Each Thursday I would join a group that spent the evening packing barrels of soap slivers, donated by New York's hotels, and crates of used clothes. Even in the early fifties, in Europe the need was still so great that no one questioned the call to gather these tiny used morsels, which we packed carefully. The others—mostly Quakers—would have a moment of silent prayer as we started to work, from which I discretely and atheistically absented myself.

Between my schoolwork, my jobs, and my volunteer activities, I had more to do than I had time for. I suspect that all this was in part to drown my father's death in a maelstrom of activity, a semblance of normalcy that gave me very little time to feel sorry for our plight or to worry about the future. On top of it all, my time at Friends was coming to an end, and I had to decide what would happen in the next four years.

No matter how poor we had been, it never occurred to me that I might not go to college. Everyone at Friends did, and so I assumed that I would, too. But the lack of money posed a major obstacle, and I was prepared to go to New York's free City College if I couldn't get a scholarship to the Ivy League schools I'd applied to. I went uptown to sit in on a CCNY class and heard the famous European historian Hans Kohn give a lecture. My only surprise was that all the students—every one of them white—were placidly eating their lunch as they listened. However, the atmosphere was pleasant enough, so I felt I had an acceptable fallback position.

Yale was, in fact, not the college I had expected to attend, but in the Spring of 1953 I went to New Haven for an interview. I paid no attention to the pleasant, tree-lined streets, nor to the anomalous, neo-Gothic college quadrangles. I was worried about my interview, not knowing what to expect. To my astonishment, the dean of admissions—a man called, appropriately enough, Whitman—ranted on at length about the kind of New York "high school trash" the University intended to exclude. I understood him to mean "New York" as a euphemism for Jews, as was common then. I felt he was either trying to provoke me to see how I would respond, or he was a hopeless anti-Semite. In any case, I felt I had to answer back and did so heatedly. I then went home assuming a future at CCNY.

Yale did eventually admit me, but they did so without offering a scholarship, which in my case amounted to a rejection. However, some friends of my parents remembered that, at Pantheon, my father had worked closely with Mary Mellon publishing the Bollingen Series of books. Mary Mellon had created the series with her husband, Paul Mellon, the multimillionaire philanthropist, son of Andrew Mellon, the former Secretary of the Treasury. He was not without influence at Yale, and a word from him sufficed to get me a full scholarship ($2,000 in those days), which not only covered the university fees but allowed me a munificent additional $400 to buy books and a celebratory ice-cream soda on Saturday night. Ironically, the old-boy network had gotten me into Yale.

As I would learn, Dean Whitman was far from atypical. In fact, Yale had a quota of only 10.1 percent Jews, which they adhered to for many more years. (The Law School, meanwhile, with an admissions policy based exclusively on merit, had a student body that was one-third Jewish.) There were a few Jewish faculty members when I arrived, which, as I was to learn, was a great improvement over the incredible anti-Semitism of the prewar period: In the twenties, the major universities, such as Yale and Harvard, had only allowed one Jewish professor per campus. Exceptions to this practice were Columbia and Berkeley… which had allowed two. [16]

---

[16] These figures come from Jerome Karabel's *The Chosen* (Boston: Houghton Mifflin, 2005), though other books have since given similar accounts of the unabashed bias of the Ivy League schools.

Yale's president, A. Whitney Griswold, had boasted in 1950 that the future Yale man—and it was all men in those days—would not be a "beetle-browed, highly specialized intellectual but a well-rounded man." This presumably excluded the notoriously intellectual Jews as well as any brainy WASPs hapless enough to apply.[17] The few Jews who were admitted came from as far away from New York as possible, and thus I became friends with people like Calvin Trillin of Kansas City, a place I had never assumed would have any Jews at all. (I found it amusing to read Andrew Hacker in a recent *New York Review of Books* quoting a *Wall Street Journal* report that some colleges were now deliberately sending recruiters to high schools with a large proportion of Jewish students.) My class also managed to have only three black members, one of whom had clearly been admitted in order to be captain of the basketball team. (By contrast, at roughly the same time—1956—Brooklyn College, one of New York City's public colleges, hired the back historian John Hope Franklin to head its history department.) In my last year at Yale, I used my position as head of the Honor Society to suggest that the group's annual project be an investigation of the school's admission policies. We were met with such a stone wall of uninterrupted lies that we had to abandon the effort.

* * *

---

[17] The other Ivy League schools were no better, according to Karabel. At Harvard, of 278 applicants from elite and predominately WASP prep schools, 245 were accepted. The acceptance rate from Exeter and Andover was 94 percent.

It wasn't until the sixties, with its new political and cultural climate, that things began to change at Yale. Kingman Brewster, who became president of Yale upon the death of Griswold in 1963, did not share the class prejudices of his predecessors. Curiously, it was one of my Yale Classmates, Inky Clark, who became the crusading new dean of admissions, and within a few years, the makeup of the undergraduate body had undergone an impressive change.

When I arrived at Yale in September of 1953 it was—not surprisingly, given its intake—hardly an exciting place intellectually. Many of the students were interested mostly in drinking and fraternity life, and they worked just hard enough to obtain George W. Bush-style "gentleman's Cs." This did not make for vibrant classroom discussions. There were, of course, many others who worked hard and wanted to get their diplomas, but they were often overshadowed by their better-prepared private school classmates.

But beyond that, McCarthyism had taken a subtler toll. There was no question of teaching any subversive doctrines. Though we were assigned Plato's *Republic* in different classes at least once every year, no one thought it worthwhile to assign or even mention Marx, nor even C. Wright Mills. The closest we came to Socialism was a class that assigned Peter Gay's *The Dilemma of Democratic Socialism: Eduard Bernstein's Challenge to Marx*. Instead, Paul Tillich and T. S. Eliot constituted the official doctrine, and the New Criticism made sure that we never went past Christian pessimism.

Our freshman English class was a model of this didacticism, and New Criticism assured that the idea that literature might have a social context was not even considered. Andover and Exeter had had the foresight to duplicate Yale's freshman curriculum in their students' final year, so their graduates already knew the party line. The rest of us had to work much harder, having never read Milton or Spenser. In class, I tried vainly to suggest that the poems of Alexander Pope sounded like a critique of English society, but I was assured that there was no such possible interpretation. Even my brilliant young instructors accepted this unquestioningly. They assigned us Cleanth Brooks, and Robert Penn Warren's *Understanding Poetry: An Anthology for College Students*, one of the seminal works of New Criticism, and it seemed the bible of the English faculty. Years later, when I went back to teach at Yale myself, I found my old freshman English teacher and asked him about the intellectual effects of McCarthy. The question clearly surprised him at first, but he gradually admitted that perhaps there had been a political subtext to the New Criticism: We had been taught that only the text mattered, and the context was irrelevant...so the possibility of literature being used to comment on its times was automatically excluded.

In the rest of the country, one could see a somewhat different ideology. From the late fifties into the sixties, a more liberal, though very cautious, approach developed. Increasingly, the works of Albert Camus and William Faulkner became core texts, particularly after Faulkner's en-Nobelment—his acceptance speech about mankind not just enduring but prevailing seemed to hit a note of response throughout the culture. The two writers, in fact, represented the same kind of cautious liberalism in response to race. Camus in Algeria and Faulkner in Mississippi had both written honestly about the issues, although they were reluctant to suggest answers or reforms. Being aware of problems seemed enough, and fitted the fifties mood perfectly.[18]

In addition to all the intellectual pressures, some of which existed in the culture as a whole, Yale was still reeling from the shock of William F. Buckley's just-published *God and Man at Yale*, in which Buckley accused the school's hidebound and conservative faculty of spreading collectivism, and he found a few textbooks that did not seem to lean sufficiently far to the right. For some reason, Buckley and his fellow conservatives were particularly down on Yale's American Studies program, which seemed to him fraught with New Deal idealism. Buckley's allies would spend a great deal of money funding student groups that would spread the word: First, they gave large amounts of money to the oddly named Inter-Collegiate Society of Individualists; later, they funded the more promising Young Americans for Freedom, a group that would eventually spearhead Barry Goldwater's takeover of the Republican party.

Meanwhile, the faculty—at least those not already on the far right—were suitably cowed. Their reluctance came from the general climate of caution and fear. I doubt very much that any faculty member knew that the FBI had a permanent office on campus to keep watch over them (and, I assume, the students)—as was revealed years later, along with the details of Yale's admission

---

[18] Later, in England, I discovered that George Orwell and E. M. Forster had played similar roles there. Their books were assigned to high school seniors—admittedly, a small part of the population (at the time, only 16 percent of students went on to take advanced A-level exams). But this enlightened minority could see that from Forster's experience in India, or Orwell's in Burma, a sensitive Englishman could understand that race was a problem, at least in the British Empire if not at home.

policies, all of which proved to have been much worse than we would have imagined back then, even in our most paranoid moments.

In addition to such marked political, ideological, and even economic pressures on both faculty and students, there was a strong social expectation of what a Yale undergraduate should become. As Lewis Lapham, the longtime editor of *Harper's Magazine* and a Yale graduate, writes in his book *Money and Class in America*, "A Yale education was a means of acquiring a cash value. Whatever the faculty said, or didn't say, what was important was the diploma. The ticket of admission to Wall Street, the professions, the safe havens of the big money." (Although I should note that Lapham, who was a year ahead of me at Yale, moved in circles of people far more social and wealthier than any I ever knew.)

We were in fact trained to enter the world of business in a myriad of indirect and often attractive ways. Those expecting to become journalists worked hard at getting onto the *Yale Daily News*, with the knowledge that a golden staircase led from there to alumni Henry Luce's Time-Life empire. Others chose less-glamorous options, such as running the student laundry—a highly remunerative job that showed managerial experience on your résumé. Most important of all was the network of secret societies, which all students hoped to join in their senior year. These were pseudo-Masonic organizations that offered mysterious rituals and a form of group therapy. Above all, they were supposed to guarantee you a cushy job upon graduation, the assurance of a comfortable life in the exclusive reaches of the real world. When in my junior year my friends and I decided that these aspects of Yale life should be challenged, we were met by incredulity. We decided to mock the tradition of "Tap Day," when juniors were "tapped" for membership in the societies, by pretending that the day was meant to center on an annual tiddlywinks tournament, which we then ostentatiously staged on the steps of the University Library. While members of the senior societies rushed around the campus, looking for the following year's members, we calmly played out our game. In the end, I was tapped for Skull and Bones, the most prestigious and notorious of the groups, the subject of many novels and films since and famous for having members such as the Presidents Bush, father and son. Our campaign against the societies had not been meant as a subtle way of trying to be asked to join, and I refused the invitation. The *Yale Daily News* subsequently ran a front-page photo of our tournament and a headline jokingly asking if I'd gone mad. Dissenting politics was one thing; rejecting a life-long certainty of prosperity was something else.

Put together, all these factors did not suggest that Yale would provide an atmosphere that would welcome with open arms a call to Socialism. Nonetheless, like a missionary among the heathens, I felt I needed to give it a try. After all, what better place than a university to use Socialism's rational and irrefutable arguments to persuade people? I had decided that the time for reading pamphlets was over, and that I should try to do something about implementing my beliefs.

* * *

In one of the pamphlets I'd picked up back at the Rand School was the mention of a student group called, unpromisingly, the Student League for Industrial Democracy. Now I wrote off to their

MY MOTHER AND ME IN 1936, A PHOTO BY THE ARTIST WOLS THAT RAN IN THE MAGAZINE *REGARDS*

ANOTHER WOLS PHOTO OF MY MOTHER AND ME; THIS ONE IS TAKEN AT THE ROYAN BEACH IN 1937.

ANDRE GIDE AND ME AT HIS COUNTRY HOME IN CUVERVILLE IN 1939

MY PARENTS WITH SARTRE DURING HIS 1945 VISIT TO NEW YORK

MY FATHER WITH HIS PARTNER, KURT WOLFF, IN THE PANTHEON OFFICES, CIRCA 1946

MY FATHER IN NEW YORK SHORTLY BEFORE HIS DEATH, LATE 1940s

NORMAN THOMAS AFTER HIS YALE ADDRESS IN 1954. I AM DIRECTLY BEHIND HIM WITH THE
OTHER MEMBERS OF THE JOHN DEWEY SOCIETY.

ONE OF THE MANY INTERNATIONAL CONFERENCES FUNDED BY THE CIA, 1957

New York address and received an encouraging batch of leaflets. The group's parent organization—the League for Industrial Democracy—had highly respectable origins, having been started in 1905 by Upton Sinclair and Jack London as the Intercollegiate Socialist Society. Somehow it had managed to survive into the fifties, a kind of American equivalent to my beloved Fabians, the British epitome of pragmatic Socialism. The LID was a lib-lab—liberal-labour—mix of old Socialists and liberals, kept going largely by the symbolic support of the old Social Democratic unions, such as the ILGWU and the United Automobile Workers (UAW).

The next time I went home to New York, I visited the old office building on East Nineteenth Street that housed not only the SLID but Norman Thomas' tiny organization, as well as the Sharecroppers Fund and other remnants of the thirties Left. I was greeted warmly by SLID's field secretary, a charming and eloquent man called Jim Farmer, who was later to become far better known as the head of the integrationist group the Congress of Racial Equality, or CORE. (Alas, he would end his days as one of Richard Nixon's few black appointees.) Jim couldn't have been more helpful or encouraging. I must have been one of the very few students to walk into that office in years, and he made no effort to conceal that the organization barely existed. I had come to discuss setting up a Yale chapter and discovered that ours would be the only branch outside New York. SLID's active membership must have numbered fewer than one hundred (in those frightened days, all the other left or liberal student groups in the country probably totaled fewer than one thousand members). Different groups used the same tricks to look more formidable than they were, such as mustering enough scattered members, many past student age, to form something that would grandly be called a regional chapter. As times got slightly better, a group of New York exiles would gather in one of the traditional havens of liberal thought—at schools such as Wisconsin, Reed, Antioch, and Berkeley—to give the impression of having a national organization. But in 1953 and '54, the pickings were very slim.

Nonetheless, I felt that I should try. The breath of McCarthyism was still sufficiently down my neck that I waited until I was eighteen and could become a naturalized citizen before venturing into student politics. I kept my French citizenship, which seemed irrelevant to me, but the threat of being deported as a radical alien seemed very real (and, in retrospect, it may have been, given the campus FBI office). Once I'd overcome the challenge of finding four more members—the minyan required by the university in order to constitute a recognized group—I settled down to the marketing problem of choosing what we would call the Yale chapter. The sheer, dated weight of SLID's name made its use impossible, but it was amazingly difficult to come up with something new that didn't make us sound like a Communist front. Words like "peace" and "democracy" were hopelessly suspect. Finally we settled on the respectable though somewhat hazy name of John Dewey, the noted founder of progressive education and a former president of the League for Industrial Democracy. Thus, SLID's Yale chapter became known as the John Dewey Society. Even with this name, however, we had the greatest difficulty finding faculty advisors willing to be identified with us. We finally got the help of two much older men, the philosopher Brand Blanchard, an old friend of Dewey's, and Carl Rollins, the University's long-retired printer and presumably a man who had

had Socialist sympathies at the turn of the century. After all this, I felt that our colors had to be nailed to a franker mast and decided to invite as our first outside speaker that old symbol of American socialism, Norman Thomas.

After considerable research in the Yale library, I found what I thought a suitable quote for a left-wing battle call, and I churned out a leaflet of embarrassing indirection, urging our follow students to "Bethink that they May be Mistaken." (Oliver Cromwell's words.) A copy of this stirring, if slightly blurred, bit of mimeography was slipped under every undergraduate's door, and we hired the Law School Auditorium in hopes of filling a respectable portion of its five hundred seats. Still, for weeks before the talk, I had nightmares that we would greet Thomas with a nearly empty hall.

The historic import of this Mickey Rooney-like story was that we filled the hall in what turned out to be the first public show of dissent at Yale in many years. Faculty members later told me how pleased they had been to see this first promise of a thaw, although I can't recall any who offered to help us at the time. Many of those who attended the meeting were too scared to put their names down afterward for the next meeting—this, just before the Army-McCarthy hearings, but at a time when the senator was under presidential attack for the first time. The townspeople—to whom we had, in good Socialist fashion, made an especially strong call—were among the most worried, and they apologized shamefacedly as they left without giving us their names. On the right, meanwhile, young followers of William F. Buckley's crusade came to picket and then later to join the audience in order to ask hostile questions. Despite his advanced age, Thomas was still an impressive speaker, his skills honed by years on the stump as the

Socialist presidential candidate. His booming pastor's voice made him seem much younger, even powerful, and the hecklers were at the mercy of the practiced wit with which he put down such objectors. I could see that many in the audience were proud of him, happy at last to hear arguments that had been largely silenced since 1948. (In the 1980s, I was invited to give a speech at a conference held at the University of Mississippi in Oxford. Afterward, several old ladies who looked as if they might well have been Faulkner's friends came up to me to say how much they'd liked my talk. One of them told me, "We haven't heard anything like this since 1948.")

The success of the event prompted a handful of other students to join our original core, including Eugene Souter, a young man who was to become the subject of newspaper headlines shortly thereafter when he renounced his family's fortune—alas, instead of donating it to the cause. But I never learned exactly what motivated our members. It's indicative of the fears at the time that one did not ask too many questions, certainly not about people's backgrounds. Of my original four comrades, one was a liberal Democrat from Danbury, Connecticut; another, I discovered years later, was the son of an old New York Communist family; the third was my Wallace-supporting classmate from Friends Seminary; and the fourth was a mysterious young man from Hartford who was to come to me the following year with his resignation, saying, in words that deserve to be immortalized: "Don't get me wrong. I still believe in the class struggle. I've just changed sides."

At the time, not only at Yale but throughout the country, SLID's tiny membership was overwhelmingly middle-class. Only in New York City was there any trace of the working class—members whose parents had been trade-union officials and who would follow in their parents' footsteps. But the idea of class differences never came up. We were united in the same cause, and that was all that mattered. Nor did we give much thought to the facts that many, though not all of us, were Jewish, and that an inordinate number of us were what was then called "Foreign-born." During the year that I was president of the national organization, two of our vice presidents, Susan Gyarmati, who continued to work for SLID, and Aryeh Neier, who was to become the head of the American Civil Liberties Union, then of Human Rights Watch, and finally of the Soros Foundation, had both been born overseas. Although undiscussed, our origins must have played an important role in our resisting the fifties political conformity that characterized the Eisenhower years. Perhaps because we all shared other loyalties, it was clearer to us—we wanted to make America something closer to the country that we had hoped to be growing up in. Perhaps, like me, the others had believed what they had been told in the forties about the changes that were to come in postwar America. (As Mary McCarthy jokes in *The Company She Keeps*, "Most men had come to socialism by some all-too-human compulsion; they were out of work or lonely or sexually unsatisfied or foreign-born....")

Most of our members have stuck to the group's ideals throughout the rest of their lives, despite becoming respectable academics. I would publish a number of them years later: Paul Chevigny, who became a leading civil-liberties lawyer and the author of several books on police abuse; Joel Kovel, known for his work on radical psychoanalysis; Jesse Lemisch, the colonial historian; and others. Joining the John Dewey Society—the JDS, as we called it—had not formed their opinions for them, but it had given them a group of like-minded classmates with whom to huddle from the cold winds of Yale's conservatism and the remnants of the McCarthy era.

But if we were nonconformists, we were far from being extremists. There were several; even tinier and more radical organizations to our left, peopled by those who joined any group of dissenters that was available. The Communists, I assume, were still largely underground. There was something called the Labor Youth League, which issued leaflets in what we considered to be nauseatingly Whitmanesque prose of excruciating vagueness. There was also the Shachtmanite group of Trotskyites (named after their charismatic leader, Max Shachtman), one of the many splinters from the original Trotskyite party. They were known primarily for the impressive weekly *Labor Action,* which was edited for years by the critic Irving Howe. They stood for a very radical "Third Camp" position, which damned both the Americans and the Russians. To my reformist mind, this seemed too much, but I went nonetheless to the vast loft on West Fourteenth Street where they were headquartered to attend their public meetings and hear what they had to say. The space was filled with lathes and other machines on which, they proudly told us, they trained members who would be sent to Detroit and elsewhere to infiltrate the unions. It was this, more than anything else, that convinced me that they were wrong: Either the workers would be swayed by their arguments or not. The idea of trying to grasp power while in disguise seemed to me immoral.[19]

There was, however, a major area in which the Shachtmanites were right and SLID was wrong. Their Third Camp line argued stridently against the U.S. and Russia alike. At SLID, we were staunchly pro-NATO, although gradually we came to espouse the European Socialist plans for a neutralized and disarmed Central Europe as an alternative to the growing Cold War and the American rearmament of Germany. England's Labour Party, led then by Hugh Gaitskell, and others felt, not unreasonably, that if the West held off rearming the Germans, the Russians might agree to a freer Eastern Europe, allowing their satellites to have the much more open status of a neutralized Austria or Finland. For a brief while, the Gaitskell-Rapacki plan looked as if it might have a chance. Had the West agreed, the Russians might have been spared the Hungarian Revolution of 1956, although our government betrayed Hungary almost as much as Russia did. (The American radio broadcasts were quick enough to urge the poor Hungarians to rebel, but we had no intention of upsetting the comfortable Cold War game in which neither side interfered in the affairs of the other.)

Nonetheless I still had faith in the European Socialist parties and their ability to counterbalance or at least moderate America's foreign policies. I can still remember a long argument with a Shachtmanite in which I argued stubbornly and stupidly that the new French Socialist government would do the right thing in

---

[19] It would be fascinating to learn more about what happened to these infiltrators and their Communist underground counterparts, but so far there has been too little written about these adventures.

Algeria. We believed as an item of faith that no Socialist government would fight a colonial war. We still held to the innocent belief that the promises of the Atlantic Charter had indeed meant something and that any delay in granting independence to the colonies was simply temporary, one that would be cleared up in time. Little did we suspect that Guy Mollet's Socialist French government would severely worsen the Algerian war, and that it would take the intervention of de Gaulle to put an end to that horrendous quagmire.

Our faith in International Socialism had a happier result closer to home. We at SLID turned to our northern neighbors and formed an alliance with the youth branch of the Cooperative Commonwealth Federation, the Canadian Socialists. We wanted to form a proper foreign policy with the CCF, so we created the grandly named North American Bureau of the International Union of Socialist Youth, a barely existing part of the barely existing Socialist International. Our first gathering was in Toronto. We went there one bitter December weekend to meet a group of charming and intelligent comrades, who had managed to do in Canada much of what we were only dreaming of in the U.S. (Interestingly, in a recent public-opinion poll in Canada asking for a list of the ten greatest Canadians, the top spot went to Tommy Douglas, the CCF head who had been largely responsible for Canada's national health service—the dreaded socialized medicine that America so feared.)

Traveling as cheaply as possible, we took the night train back to New York, and on reaching the border we found ourselves awakened in the darkened train and confronted by agents of the FBI. They questioned us closely about our meetings with the CCF, about which they appeared to be fully informed, although there had been no public announcements of our plans. Finally, they let us complete our journey home.

We were neither surprised nor frightened by this. We had lived so long with the expectation of FBI surveillance that when they finally came and questioned us it was somewhat anticlimactic. Yet thinking back, one has to marvel at the amount of work that must have gone into their ability to pick us out from the hundreds of drowsy passengers. How many secret photos must have been taken, how many phones tapped, how many letters intercepted? All to watch a perfectly innocent and legitimate gathering of ultra-loyal Social Democrats.

* * *

By my third year of college politics, my extracurricular work with SLID was beginning to resemble a full-time job. By my senior year, I had joined a program that exempted us from regular classes in exchange for writing a senior thesis. For my subject I had chosen the Riom trial of Léon Blum by the Vichy government, and that government's failed attempt to blame the Third Republic for France's defeat and in general to smear French democrats. I was fascinated by what had happened to those left behind whose views I shared.

Working on the thesis, however, gave me a lot of free time to try to bring Social Democracy to the United States. Late at night in my Yale room I would type up endless encouraging newsletters chronicling our many successes throughout the country's campuses. SLID was expanding impressively. We now numbered in the hundreds and could count a respectable group of chapters across the country, chapters that were becoming more active and aggressive. In Wisconsin, for example, the group had challenged an ongoing witch hunt by the local American Legion, asking them to supply the same information about funding and officers that they sought from other groups. This seemed too aggressive to the college paper, the *Daily Cardinal*, which suggested that SLID was just out for publicity and that since SLID's stated aims included the nationalization of basic industries, we were hardly in a position to challenge others.

At Yale, our activities were less provocative and more conventional. Our meetings drew bigger and bigger crowds. The topics ranged from discussions of national health insurance to a defense of the Communist victims of the Smith Act. The latter talk was given by the Yale law professor Thomas Emerson, a Progressive Party member who would not have gotten a hearing elsewhere. We even invited Communist historian Herbert Aptheker to speak, although we carefully labeled him as a Communist spokesman. I invited speakers whose appeal went beyond our basic audience, such as Hannah Arendt and Dwight MacDonald. MacDonald was a classic example of someone who had gone from Yale to Henry Luce's empire, in this case *Fortune* magazine. Once there, he wrote brilliant articles that did not always toe the party line. He became most famous during the war, when he launched a tiny journal called *Politics,* which spoke out against the overwhelming support of the war. He published people such as the pacifist Simone Weil, and became notorious for attacking our use of atomic bombs on the Japanese. MacDonald had not been back to Yale since his own undergraduate days in the thirties and had kept a very sour memory of that time. He was astonished to find our small group of leftists and was delighted, as were we, to meet. He and I became lifelong friends as a result, but it was only years later—when I read a *New York Times* homage to his centennial—that I realized that this feisty and witty man had been a good thirty years older than I.

But if SLID represented dissent on domestic issues, our meetings on foreign policy might not have been out of place at the Council of Foreign Relations (and may indeed have been replicated there). Our foreign-policy speakers included such Cold Warriors as Zbigniew Brzezinski and David Dallin, and our discussions got approving front-page attention in the college paper and elsewhere. For a panel on the Vietnam War, we primarily sought official speakers from the French and Vietnamese governments. Ironically, our attempts to bring in other views often enough resulted in our inviting people who were—unbeknownst to us—already working with the CIA. We would discover in time that the CIA had been very efficient in recruiting former Trotskyite and other Communist dissidents who, in turn, were happy to continue their battles against Stalin and his successors under the CIA's auspices.

But our acceptance at Yale went well beyond the growing attendance at meetings of the John Dewey Society. Gradually, the campus seemed to see our presence as a normal part of university life, not as a marginal, subversive activity. I'm sure this was due as much to the general thaw in American life as to the special circumstances at Yale, but still, the JDS was clearly adding something of value to the university's intellectual life. The respectable pro-Cold War programs far outweighed the more radical ones. The college newspaper covered us respectfully. I no longer needed to worry about empty auditoriums, and an ever-increasing number of students joined our ranks.

As individuals, we became much more integrated into the university's cultural and intellectual life. Many of my friends and fellow JDS stalwarts also became members of the Elizabethan Club, Yale's intellectual gathering place. There, the various factions gathered for tea—the politically committed from both sides, the aesthetes, the intellectuals. We all welcomed the chance to meet and talk outside the narrow framework of classes and fraternities. I became a book reviewer for the *Yale Daily News*, though I never felt I belonged to that close-knit group. In my senior year, I was asked to head the Aurelian Honor Society, part of Yale's elite. I won various oratorical prizes (remnants of Yale's nineteenth-century heritage), and became part of the scene. In short, while we objected to many of Yale's values, we were certainly able to enjoy its pleasures. In the end, I graduated summa cum laude and was chosen to give the graduation address. Much more important, I received the Snow Prize, given to "the man who has done the most for Yale," which came with several thousand much-needed dollars to give to my mother. By that point she was working as a designer in the city but earning very little; the prize money was equal to several months of her salary.

* * *

My life was also to change as a result of getting one of the two annual Clare Fellowships to Cambridge University. The money was given annually by Paul Mellon, who wanted to let others experience the life he had led himself after going from Yale to Clare, one of the older colleges making up the university. Each year the fellowship also sent two Englishmen to my own Yale college. The grant was munificent enough to allow me to live in considerable luxury while in England, but I would still work in New York in the summer to continue to contribute to the family finances.

During my last year at Yale and before leaving for England, I reverted to a full-time commitment to the cause. During school vacations I spent an increasing amount of time in the LID office on East Nineteenth Street, mimeographing numerous reports and pamphlets. In the summer, after working all day at a job on Wall Street, I would go back and labor well into the night. This was before everyone had air conditioning, and LID's offices seemed literally like a sweatshop, rather than the center of social change. I kept poor Jim Farmer at work for endless hours, printing a series of pamphlets that were, in effect, my entry into the world of publishing. I enjoyed this experiment in publishing and worked hard at making the pamphlets known. I got them listed in *Publishers Weekly* and the *Library Journal,* just like real books. I even wrote a circular to leading libraries offering the first five for a mere dollar. The pamphlets were more my priority than SLID's, though some managed to have a slight influence on the Left's debates.

SLID had concentrated largely on domestic issues, but although it took me many years to figure it out, it was our foreign-policy stance that began to interest other organizations (besides the FBI). Our solid anti-Communist position had made us respectable nationally, and we could summon a number of genuine campus leaders who looked and sounded good in a public forum. In addition to that, with the waning of McCarthyism, our ideas were becoming more acceptable, even popular.

Finally, SLID was invited to participate in a national coordinating committee of the country's various youth groups, from the YMCA to the Students for Democratic Action, our liberal-democrat counterparts. The aims of the group that invited us were vague, but we were so pleased with the invitation that we asked few further questions. As president of SLID, I found myself invited to gatherings in the Carnegie Endowment building, right next to the United Nations. We met in impressive conference rooms and my colleagues and I found that people were willing to listen to our arguments. Indeed, a number of delegates from the other organizations decided to join SLID, and when the time came to elect delegations to go to international meetings, we were high in the balloting. Our newsletter filled up with these accomplishments, showing our growing role domestically and internationally.

Perhaps it was SLID's relative political sophistication, our eloquence, our genuine idealism, or simply the appeal of anti-Communism with a human face, but I soon found myself in an increasing number of delegations traveling to meetings in Europe. Theoretically, we were dealing with the social and political issues facing young people throughout the world; at least, that's what we were told by the meetings' organizers. My first gathering in 1956 was in a still-devastated Berlin. I was astonished to see that the city had hardly been rebuilt, and most of the new buildings were, at most, two stories tall. The meetings were rather boring, and some of my colleagues and I were tempted to explore the whole city, which, in those pre-Wall days, was still completely accessible. East Germany's workers had revolted just a few years before, in 1953, and we wondered whether we could find out what people actually felt. My high school German would finally be of use, I thought. We were delighted when we were lured to East Berlin by a group of stunningly inept young Communists who came up to talk to us. We had hoped to get some idea of what their life was like, but instead, they apparently had instructions to drive us around the city and point out the danger of traffic accidents caused by the presence of the occupying American forces, which they seemed to think would persuade us to urge American troops to leave. That was all they had apparently been told to talk about—all other conversation proved impossible. Their side certainly did not seem better than ours at the ideological battles of the Cold War.

The next year, at a meeting in Rome of youth groups from the NATO countries, I discovered that my fellow Socialists were expected to form a fraction, or caucus, in which we would hammer out a common policy. I was given the task of finding wording that would be acceptable both to the French and Algerian delegates. Having written so many upbeat newsletters, I had no trouble finding the vague and uplifting language that both sides could accept.

It was in Rome, it must be admitted, that I noted a few of my fellow "youth leaders" looked past their prime. All of the British delegation were in its forties and dressed like middle-aged gentlemen. The Portuguese delegates were all clearly government bureaucrats. This did not worry me unduly. After all, I realized that other countries lacked our great pluralistic tradition of voluntary organizations. It was for this reason that the others tended to look somewhat portly and had heavy five o'clock shadows. Downy cheeked as we were, we represented the fresh-faced and energetically involved youth of our country, the very people who would in time join the Kennedy administration. In the meantime we convincingly gave the lie to the impression that America had bred a frightened and silent generation.

In 1957, my last year in college, I was asked by the seemingly respectable Foundation for Youth and Student Affairs, the organization that had helped to fund all these gatherings, whether I would be willing to go to Vienna during the Communist World Youth Festival. The U.S. had decided to send a large anti-Communist delegation. However, I would be working with the Socialist Youth International, whose headquarters were in Vienna, writing and preparing whatever propaganda I deemed most effective. My naiveté let me be persuaded by the Foundation's argument that Europe's Socialists were still too close to their colonialist views to do this effectively. We Americans, on the other hand, represented a proud commitment to colonial liberation. The fact that we would also be much more reliable Cold Warriors was not mentioned nor did it ever occur to me.

A salary check for $150 per week was deposited directly into my New York bank account; therefore I would later have no paper trail of who had paid me or why. This didn't trouble me at the time, it merely seemed simple and convenient. Unlike the American group, led by Gloria Steinem and others, who had gone to defend our foreign policy, I could adhere to the Socialist line opposing both the colonialists and the Russians, and I came perilously close to the Shachtmanite arguments I had rejected so vociferously in the past. My posters and pamphlets argued against France's Algerian and Vietnamese wars, as well as against the

Soviet repression in Hungary. We protested the continued colonial domination of much of the Third World, even though the European Socialists were slow to do so. I was wrongly not quite ready to praise the Bandung alliance, in which neutralists such as Nehru, Tito, and Nasser had tried to create a genuine Third Way, but I was sympathetic to whatever other alternatives to capitalism and communism seemed politically possible.

Vienna was still very poor and dreary in 1957, looking much more like the setting of *The Third Man* than like the overly affluent city it has since become. I had no trouble renting a room from an impoverished old lady who lived alone in a sprawling, dusty, and ill-lit apartment in one of the old palaces that filled the center of town. I worked unceasingly with my comrades from the International Union of Socialist Youth and the Austrian Socialist Party. Doing our best, working late into the night, we churned our endless pamphlets and posters arguing for the Socialist alternative.

I realized only later that the tiny amounts of money given me to pay for these pamphlets, always late and often inadequate, was a thimbleful compared to the torrents of cash given to the "official" Americans—the groups sent as the American delegates to the youth festival. Their daily newspaper defended America's foreign policy consistently, and the French version even boasted of the number of Algerian rebels killed every day. My efforts were drowned out by this torrent of pro-Western propaganda.

Evelyn Waugh warns in *Brideshead Revisited* that "It is easy, retrospectively, to endow one's youth with. . . a false innocence," but I fear that all of us were genuinely innocent. We believed what we were told and were puzzled by the contradictions, but still, we never suspected what was actually going on.

Several years later, I discovered that our presence at the

Vienna "Youth Festival" had been a CIA con job. They had paid for all our joint activities at the Festival, even my posters denouncing the colonialists. The Socialist Youth International had been on their payroll as well. The American youngsters in Vienna had been real enough, but the rest was flimflam. The international organizations we met with, with grand names like the World Assembly of Youth, had been created to combat groups that the Soviets had created—our group was the counterpart to their World Federation of Democratic Youth, and other groups were created to offset their efforts with students, workers, lawyers, you name it.

Most of the foreign delegates at our international conferences were indeed government bureaucrats, who masqueraded as youth leaders. We were important because we provided ideal window dressing for the CIA shop. Our Potemkin conferences could be used to counter the Soviet efforts. But more important, they could fool the genuine youth leaders from Third World countries. Charmed by our liberalism and anticolonial rhetoric, they could be beguiled and gradually sucked onto the CIA payroll. Since in many of these countries the steps between being a student leader and a government minister were relatively few, the CIA could easily gather and recruit important future links. Nor was this limited to candidates from the Third World—in time I would discover that a number of British organizations and even MPs from all parties were on the CIA payroll as well. We, the liberal and Socialist members of the Western delegations, proved to be the ideal fig leaves for the real work of intelligence and bribery that was our hidden agenda.

It took me a long while to cotton on. I was offered jobs with some conservative groups that I suspected might be linked to our government, and I rejected these indignantly—only to discover later that my work in Vienna had been paid for from the same CIA purse. Here we were in Vienna denouncing the Soviets because their youth groups were controlled by their government, because their society precluded the possibility of pluralism, that sacred word of the fifties . . . and we were not bright enough to have realized that our own government had used us to give the impression of a far more pluralistic America than actually existed. Like Adlai Stevenson covering up Kennedy's invasion of Cuba at the U.N., we were far better liars for having been completely sincere. Many of our elders and betters were also being used by the CIA in the same way. It amazed me to read statements by Stephen Spender, the editor of the CIA-funded *Encounter* magazine, who claimed that they, too, had been misled; I found this hard to believe. Even our beloved Norman Thomas had knowingly chosen to work with the CIA at the time of the Hungarian Revolution and had cooperated with CIA efforts to bring the Hungarian Socialist leaders to America. At Yale we organized a protest that filled the vast Wolsey Auditorium to listen to the Hungarian socialist leader Anna Kethley denounce the Russian repression.

The whole sordid story of the CIA's use of the Left and others would come out in the sixties in the radical American magazine *Ramparts,* and later in a book that I published called *The Cultural Cold War,* a very thorough history by the British filmmaker Frances Stoner Saunders. One of the first exposés appeared on March 4, 1967, in the *New Republic,* which reported, "Hiding behind seemingly independent fronts, the CIA got a great deal for its money. When it wanted to bring European socialists into its 'safe' world student groups, it used a small American socialist—but anti-Communist organization, the Student League for Industrial Democracy—as bait. The CIA-funded Young Adult Council invited the socialists to join the Council. SLID did, thinking it had made a real political breakthrough. Thereafter the CIA could point to the fact that the 'free' American socialists were part of the show, so why didn't their European counterparts join Agency-financed world student organizations." But this was really just icing on the cake.

At the very same time, the *New Republic* pointed out, the CIA was hard at work on its basic agenda, conniving to promote the overthrow of governments in the Western Hemisphere that were too independent of U.S. influence—financing strikes against the independent leftist Cheddi Jagan in Guyana, for example. And not just strikes: The CIA funded terrorist groups that "blew up government buildings," the *New Republic* reported, "bombed merchant ships in the Georgetown harbor and beat up the citizenry. Explosives, guns and ammunition were distributed freely to a 600 man private army ready to seize control of Georgetown if a general strike failed." It was, in other words, the old, familiar pattern that had succeeded in Guatemala and would continue to be enacted throughout Central America—seen most recently in the successful American efforts to dislodge Jean-Bertrand Aristide in Haiti, and in our less successful efforts to overthrow Hugo Chavez in Venezuela.

It is reasonable to conclude from all this that the help we gave—however indirectly—to our government's foreign policy far outweighed whatever harm we could possibly have done at home. It was not until well into the Vietnam War that the massive and unified support that the government had enjoyed for its foreign policy since the Second World War began to falter. What little political debate existed focused overwhelmingly on domestic issues. There, the growing thaw did make a difference. By the time I graduated from Yale in June of 1957, the fearful climate of the early fifties had largely dissipated. More and more people were willing to join us and other groups on the left. The conformity, the silence, had begun to crack.

But the major changes that were taking place came from a source with which we had very little to do and for which we could take no credit. Starting in 1955 with the Montgomery bus boycott, the civil rights movement became an ever-increasing force for sweeping social change. Truman had made some important progress in integrating the armed forces, and even Eisenhower had been forced, if reluctantly, to send in troops to protect the students integrating the schools in Little Rock. History had taken over from us and moved events much faster than we had ever thought possible.

* * *

On graduating from Yale, I moved to England to begin my two-year Mellon Fellowship, and the time had come for me to stop my involvement in American student politics. Being in England would allow me to easily continue to attend my international meetings, however, and I could finally join the Fabians and see what the Labour Party was up to. But the move would clearly bring about a break with my activities of the preceding four years.

The young people who were beginning to join SLID were smart and impressive, but they were no longer interested in the same issues that had been central to us. Changing the government's basic economic policies, nationalizing industries, even extending the welfare state, did not seem possible any more. To be sure, industrial democracy could be repackaged as "workers' control" or "participatory democracy," but no one expected workers to actually run factories, and no one had even heard of Guild Socialism.

It seemed time to redo the image of SLID, so in 1957 I came up with a number of new names, which I sent out on a postcard for our members to vote on. The most popular choice, by far, was "Students for a Democratic Society"—SDS. The youngsters who were joining SDS and would take over—the Tom Haydens, Al Habers, et al.—were much more pragmatic and populist than we had been. They were also mostly American—and not, for the most part, the offspring of immigrants—and very few were Jews. They seemed more autochthonous—more the traditional home-grown radicals of the American past. It seemed to me that their politics would be more mainstream, more conservative.

Equally important, things were beginning to move much more quickly in the universities. Our immediate successors in SDS were very different people than we had been. For the most part, these new leaders came from campus politics, like the National Students Association (NSA). Though at first their politics seemed more conservative, more American to me, they felt that they had abandoned our narrower, more old-fashioned approach. They were interested in broader, campus-oriented issues that would link them to many of their contemporaries. They had no sympathy for our Fabianism, our addiction to social engineering. They understood the folly of our expectations—there would be no grand coalition, no help from the unions and the masses. In time, though, they would find new allies where we had not dared hoped they might exist.

It is useful to look at Tom Hayden's memoirs in this respect. Hayden was barely aware of his predecessors, referring to SLID as one of the groups that had "flourished in the thirties but flickered out by the McCarthy period... they tended to be confined to students who were from Jewish, immigrant, New York backgrounds," he wrote, not without a certain disdain.[20] With Al Haber, he hoped in 1960 to start a new organization, "now to be renamed SDS," completely unaware that we had done this some three years before, and that SDS had already grown impressively throughout the country. But Hayden was right in feeling that he was doing something new. Unlike the gray immigrants in New York, he would in time be elected to the legislature of sunny California and work there effectively for many years, something that none of us would have thought possible (not to mention marrying Jane Fonda). In time, Hayden would also discover his own immigrant roots and work imaginatively with the warring youth factions in Ireland, as he would in his native Los Angeles. Recently, I suggested to him that he write about this for The New Press.

---

[20] Hayden, Reunion (New York: Random House,1988), 29-30.

In addition to this, a new kind of cultural dissent had begun to appear. With the publication of Jack Kerouac's novel *On the Road*, what became known as the Beat Generation flourished in the new coffeehouses on college campuses and throughout the country's major cities. Some of the fifties social and sexual conformity was challenged (though Kerouac himself was not ready to admit to his bisexuality). The Beats were attractive and titillating after the gray Eisenhower years, but they were not dangerous politically. *Life* magazine was among the first to celebrate them—which made me realize how easily and quickly they could be absorbed into the mainstream culture.

In my last speech as SDS president in 1957, I chose the *Life* article as my theme, to show how quickly America could absorb and neuter some forms of dissent. (Later, Tom Frank would describe something similar in *The Conquest of Cool*, his book on how Madison Avenue had learned to turn sixties slogans into advertising mantras.) My fear was that the seeming conservatism of the new generation of leftists would merge with the establishment's blandishments and put an end to the old Socialist hopes for a transformed society once and for all.

In any event, in spite of the Beats, as the fifties ended the Eisenhower consensus was still very much in place. The country was prosperous, wages had gone up steadily since the war's end, more and more blacks were moving from the lowest pay scales to decent jobs in industry. There seemed very little need for a Left, old or new. I could only hope that England, and Europe, would offer a different world.

When I was an undergraduate at Yale, the ancient British universities of Oxford and Cambridge were always spoken of in a special tone of voice. They represented the Kingdom of Heaven to our lonely, puritan outpost. They were the earthly paradise on which we sought to model ourselves, physically and spiritually. Just as men had sought to imagine God's appearance by knowing that he had created man in his image, so we could picture what Cambridge and Oxford were like by looking at our own colleges and from them projecting the real university.

Every few years, a delegation of Yale officials would make a pilgrimage to the Holy Land and return with relics of the College System and Individual Supervisions. Speeches would be made, reports written—interspersed with little jokes about rolling lawns for five hundred years—and then decisions would be made: A college library would be expanded, an optional course would be allowed. As I left Yale in 1957, I remember a great deal of attention being spent on the college seals that appeared on our china and notepaper. A decision had been made to emblazon the entrance to each college with a large version of its seal, and when I returned to New Haven several years later, these escutcheons had become part of the university's life—the gilt already tarnished by time and weather, ever closer to the wonder and splendor of the British originals.

It is difficult at this remove to recapture entirely the amaze-ment, awe, and anticipation with which I learned in my senior year that I had been granted an exchange fellowship to Cambridge. The Clare grants always brought two Cambridge men to Yale from Clare College and one of them always lived in Berkeley, my Yale college. Over the years, I had come to know these terribly pleasant, amiable men, who for the most part did not seem exceptionally interested in studying but sought, with great charm and energy, to become acquainted with American life. They could be easily distinguished by the leisurely pace at which they lived and the daring with which they installed electric hot plates in their rooms, so that they could serve instant coffee at all hours of day and night. (Such instruments were strictly for-bidden by university rules, and special room inspectors would periodically ferret them out. Somehow, perhaps by the brazen-ness with which the English left their contraband lying about, they were never penalized.)

Having known these men and, after all, having seen various photos of Cambridge over the years, I should have had some idea of what to expect. But I realized that I hadn't the faintest idea of what this world would look like. Just as Milton failed to give us useful visions of Paradise, so all my projections and images failed me. I rushed to the Sterling Library and exhausted its stock on Cambridge: one picture book, a couple of sports histories, and a Cambridge Press history of one of the colleges. I read *Jacob's Room*, Virginia Woolf's novel set in Cambridge, and the Cambridge undergraduate newspaper, but nothing helped. Finally, I resigned myself to discovering the pragmatic details that were to govern my existence. I wrote to Yale men, barely known, already there, who instructed me to bring sheets—but no blankets—and a minimum of electric appliances. I knew that it would be cold, that the natives would be aloof, that I would probably be continuing my work in history. But that was all.

I was, of course, worried about leaving Simone alone, but I planned to come back the following summer, both to earn more money and to keep her company. So, in September of 1957, she joined my Yale friends in seeing me off on the Mauretania, the old Cunard liner that took me across the Atlantic in slightly greater luxury than I had known on my liberty ship, eight years before.

* * *

I arrived in London, and I got up early the following morning to take the train to Cambridge. I felt I had no time to lose, not even a morning to spare for sightseeing in London. I arrived early at the Liverpool Street station and stood outside it for a while, looking at the passing crowd. After a while I burst out laughing at how identical everyone seemed: Endless young men in bowler hats and carrying wrapped umbrellas; young women, all tidily dressed for the day's work; all of them white—there was none of New York's variety, a far cry from today's multicultural London.

Much as I wanted to know more about London, I felt that I should get to Cambridge a few days early to acquaint myself with my new college and its surroundings. I suppose I felt like all new boys at school, cosmically behind everyone else and desperately in need of catching up—with what, I wasn't sure. But I had no time to lose, certainly not a morning to spare for sightseeing.

I waited impatiently for the train to reach Cambridge; it took exactly the hour and seventeen minutes required to go from New York to New Haven. The Cambridge station looked like any small-town station; I later learned that it was the longest platform in England because the Cambridge authorities had initially agreed to allow only one track to desecrate their city. My cab carried me down a highway totally free of historical monuments except for a First World War statue near the station, and I soon reached a deserted complex of "contemporary" buildings, which had been built in the twenties. On one side of me was a vast, factorylike skyscraper that vaguely resembled Stanford's Hoover Institute, the university's library. Opposite was a huge four-story quadrangle of gray stone, which to my Yale-trained eyes seemed more appropriate to some quintessential Midwestern university. I didn't dare ask the cab driver whether he had made some horrible mistake. Yes, this was Clare College, the Memorial Court, built after the First War at some distance and across the river Cam from the old Clare building.

I made my way to the porter's lodge and there was greeted by an elderly servant, similar in appearance to the retired cops who used to patrol the Yale colleges, but infinitely more obsequious. Yes, indeed, my rooms were ready. I had arrived a little early (I must have been the only person in the whole college), but the others would soon be coming up. I expected to be handed an envelope full of welcome, instruction, and orientation, but was given only my key and the directions to my rooms. I had been put, I discovered, in the most modern part of the building. With touching solicitude, the college authorities had placed all of us Latin-types, Americans, West Indians, Africans, and Asians in the one unit endowed with central heating. (This was, of course, still an unnatural phenomenon in England and the architects had placed the pipes that were to replace radiators so deep inside the walls that the rooms themselves were rarely heated, though we suspected that the outside of the building was probably nice and cozy.)

My rooms, for they were indeed in the plural, overwhelmed me. I had, to myself, a sitting room with (I counted them immediately) no fewer than seven chairs, plus a bedroom of my own and the shared use of a kitchen and bathroom (with bath). At Yale, with great good luck, I had in my last years landed a single room, which contained the two wooden chairs allotted as a maximum. I could hardly believe Cambridge's luxury, the lavishness. Some of the furniture was upholstered, and the décor, though hardly to my taste, would have done credit to any second-rank hotel. The period was Festival modern, the style of fifties Britain, which, from the lettering on better men's rooms to the design of the Festival Hall, bespoke the virtues of a nation that was smart, careful, that knew where it stood and, having survived the Blitz, was now determined to treat itself a little.

Gradually I was to discover how carefully planned all of this had been. The kitchens were not there so that we could cook our own meals—as we were soon to do to avoid the incredibly bad food which the college apparently has always served—but so that we could make our own breakfast (light frying was allowed) and entertain guests. Yale's prohibition of hot plates had been equally well planned. Breakfast was served until 8:25, and we all knew that we had to be up by 8:23 or pay exorbitantly to eat out. Yale thus used this economic whip to force us to get up at a reasonable hour, whereas Clare, by allowing us to opt out of breakfast and have butter, milk, and loaves of unwrapped English bread delivered to our doorsteps as a matter of course, positively encouraged a sybaritic way of life. Likewise the number of chairs encouraged having people in for tea, coffee, or drinks at all hours, and even the electric heater that happily, supplemented the central heating was constructed so that one could toast bread and crumpets with ease.

By the end of my first few weeks, I realized what was going on. I had stumbled on a rather anachronistic two-star hotel housed in one of the historic English estates that one read about. My fellow guests were pretty much what you would expect in the circumstances: incredibly friendly. After all, why go to a resort if not to meet new people? Far from being aloof, they stumbled over each other to invite you to coffee, tea, sherry, or after-dinner drinks (which could be bought in the bar that the college had conveniently installed in the crypt under the chapel), or even to share a friendly glass of beer or cider at dinner, the purchase of which the college encouraged by serving only lukewarm water of its own accord. All the guests, even those on state scholarships (90 percent, after all) had enough money to be able to invite you or to reciprocate.

The hotel provided a well-rounded program of activities. The physical plant may not have been up to Yale standards; Berkeley had its own billiards room, for instance, in addition to an excellent library, a good music room, and so forth. But Clare made up for these lacks with an excellent athletic schedule. As far as I could ascertain, my fellow guests would go off every afternoon to play games, coming back at teatime dirty, exhausted, but clearly the better for it. They would have a good hearty tea, and I can still see the college at dusk, a merry electric fire blazing in every room and surrounded by drying sports uniforms and happy young faces tucking into tea and toast. This was an important part of the day: It offered needed rest after a major effort and also filled the stomach so that the inadequate evening meal could pass relatively unnoticed. After-dinner coffee filled the time before the evening's incredible array of extracurricular activities; vastly more than what we at Yale had ever seen. The university's library, which might have tempted someone to read some book or other, considerately closed before suppertime (though it had its own, excellent tearoom). The evening passed, everyone would be in bed well before midnight. One night when some fellow Americans and I worked until dawn preparing a special issue of the undergraduate newspaper, we found ourselves periodically visited by dons (the faculty in residence in the college), porters, and students, making sure that we were all right, that our mad scheme was not endangering our health. Working through the night was a common practice at Yale, but I still remember seeing one of my Cambridge friends at exam time, swollen-eyed and miserable, explaining that he had been forced to stay up past midnight.

As can be seen, this schedule left very little free time. There was still the period between breakfast and lunch—minus the eleven-o'clock coffee break during which every café and restaurant in Cambridge was full of students. (One town hotel offered well-attended afternoon tea dances, though I never checked to see whether morning coffee dances were held or who attended them.) With some careful planning and a good bicycle, one could, if one wished, attend two, possibly three lectures a day. These were conveniently scheduled in the morning, so as not to interfere with games, though scientist friends did tell me that some lab work had to be done in the afternoon. Attendance at lectures was voluntary and, of course, much commoner among beginning students and at the beginning of the year.

In spite of this, the undergraduate program made heavy demands, and the lecturers included the world-famous academicians for which Cambridge was known. (In my own field, there were far more European historians than in Yale's college and graduate school put together.) In addition to attending lectures, students were expected to meet with a teacher for a fortnightly "supervision," an hour-long discussion of a set subject on which the student had written a brief essay.

Though I had received my BA from Yale, I did not want to register for the doctoral program, and the aim of my scholarship had been to let me participate in the undergraduate life. I therefore enrolled in a special two-year program, designed for visiting Americans, more intensive than that of my English counterparts, which would lead to the equivalent of the American MA. I could attend any lectures I wished, primarily those on subjects which were to constitute my exams, and I would have three supervisions a fortnight—in effect, write an essay and prepare a discussion every five days. Here at last I felt that I would see the heart of the Cambridge program, the faculty and the miraculous system of supervisions which Yale had so often wished to emulate.

* * *

Within a few months, I was at my wit's end. My supervision topics were of such overwhelming scope that I could hardly begin to cope with them, much less write about them, in my five days.

Finally, the fortnight came when I had to write about alienation in Marx and Hegel, the economic causes of the French Revolution, and the effects of the Great Reform Bill. I balked and refused to continue. This was worse than the worst book-skimming and lecture-regurgitation that I had faced at Yale. The whole academic process seemed a shambles. I had been attending my lectures faithfully, and they seemed no better than those at Yale. The supervisions had likewise proved anticlimactic. It was unlikely that you would find the right man for you among the college fellows to whom you were sent. As likely as not, you landed a very nice man who felt that he was wasting your time, or you his. Occasionally the supervisions were farmed out to graduate students, their BA's fresh on their walls. (I once visited the apartment of one of these on a Saturday morning and was greeted by a voluptuous brunette in a scarlet dressing gown. "Are you here for a supervision?" she asked politely.)

The basic problem lay with the curriculum. Students had three years in which to whiz over vast areas at the speed suggested by my decisive fortnight. To be sure, it had been an unhappy conjunction. I might have had the English political philosopher T. H. Greene to master instead of Marx and he could have been done in four days. Some of the other topics had been assigned so often that your supervisor (or fellow students) could tell you which articles, rather than which books, to read. But all of this was cheating, and it was no way for a university to behave. It was, in any case, not what I had come to Cambridge for and I said so to my supervisor. I had, after all, one degree and hardly needed an MA. I wanted out—to read at my own pace and spend whatever time I wanted on my assignments. Everyone agreed. I could do whatever I wanted.

Spring arrived along with my newfound freedom, and I soon discovered that what I wanted to do bore little relation to spending more time on the Great Reform Bill. The weather was unbelievable. After a Cambridge winter, I had never suspected that spring could have the warmth and softness of the Riviera. The exquisite Clare gardens were in bloom, and my friends and I spent the morning sunning ourselves and reading. With a picnic basket and a bottle of sweet English cider you could even forget that teatime was approaching. The country around Cambridge is still marvelously unspoiled, made for walking, and a total contrast to New Haven, where a determined afternoon's exploring brought forth only endless suburban streets.

Other activities soon imposed themselves, and even other disciplines. I discovered that I had to get up quite early on a Saturday morning to have the first look at the old-book stall in the weekly town market. My housekeeping cares had grown as I increasingly avoided college meals. My fellow Americans and I would exchange careful dietetic advice on how to avoid scurvy within a modest budget; oranges were prohibitively expensive but grapefruit were reasonable, and when in season, Belgian endives could make up for the total lack of fresh greens in our institutional diet.

I spent my monthlong spring vacation in Italy, visiting Florence and Rome each for the first time and discovering the country's incredible charm and beauty. I returned to Cambridge to find that most of the students had retreated to their homes to put in a month's hard work. The Cambridge academic year is all of twenty-six weeks long, more than two months shorter than the Yale year. Most Cambridge students were on grants and therefore did not need vacation work and could devote their vacations to study. Home was obviously so boring compared with Cambridge that there was little else for them to do.

By the end of the first year, I had established my own, highly comfortable modus vivendi. I had begun to meet students from other colleges, had come to know several dons on an informal, amicable basis, and had resigned myself to the suspicion with which my Cold War ideas were viewed by other members of the Labour Club, which I had immediately joined. I had settled down to reading many of the books that I'd never had time for at Yale. I was spending less time writing unhappy letters home and more time writing for the various undergraduate papers. Though I didn't quite understand how Cambridge worked, I no longer felt like an uncomfortable outsider. I had my work, the others had theirs. It was to take a second year for me to realize what Cambridge was really all about.

* * *

I had to return to America to work during that summer, continuing my summer work at New American Library, the paperback house where I got my first publishing job. So Cambridge looked doubly enchanting when I returned from New York. We were in our last year and had the confident familiarity of all seniors. I thought back on the visiting American historian who'd come for a year and toward the end had confided: "Obviously some kind of learning process goes on here, but I'll be damned if I know what it is." A year, clearly, had been inadequate, and many of my compatriots, over for only one year, had soon given up and retreated to their rooms.

I had banded together with the other Americans who were in Clare for their second year, and the college authorities, who would normally have frowned on such cliquishness, must have realized that we were acting from simple animal instinct of survival. In our second year, we had taken the option of moving back to the lovely old Clare building in spite of its lack of central heating, and we began to plan for the winter as Admiral Perry must have. (At one point, when heat from our gas fire failed utterly to reach back into our bedrooms, we petitioned to be allowed to use paraffin (kerosene) stoves, which were finally forbidden to us on the very reasonable grounds that they could have gutted the college's wooden interior. But for a brief moment, comfort seemed within sight. "Those stoves are marvelous," the college's secretary had told us. "They bring the temperature right up there into the forties.")

Apart form the cold, life was extraordinarily graceful. Our vast rooms looked out over the Clare courtyard as well as the King's College backs, with a view of the Cam and of King's Chapel. It was like living in a palace. Our last puritanical reflexes disappeared. We awoke to a leisurely breakfast and the *Guardian*, banished all lectures before ten a.m., returned for a simple little lunch prepared in our rooms or occasionally taken at some pub, kept ample supplies of cocoa and of eggs for scrambling in the late evening when, locked in the college, we had to rely on our own stores. (Not that scaling the wall, as most undergraduates did, would have helped at this time, since Cambridge closed most of its doors at eleven p.m. in any case.) The need to leave at night seemed minimal, our existence hopelessly monastic. True, there were three women's colleges in the university, but for the most part, their inhabitants were very forbidding. Soon after I left, the miracle of Mary Quant and the miniskirt made Cambridge something of a fashion center, but in our times there were incredibly few pretty girls, and they apparently embarked on interminable affairs their first week. Nor did it seem very hopeful to haunt the large number of schools that purported to teach English to an endless gaggle of pretty bourgeois foreign girls. One felt that even a fluent mastery of Swedish or Dutch would elicit no more than the constant giggling we heard issuing from the Jaguars and MGs of the heirs of minor sheikdoms and defunct Italian baronetcies who had somehow gained entrance to one of the more careless Cambridge colleges. Perhaps our very resignation put us above the fray and brought us the one thing that we felt Cambridge had denied us: genuine English girlfriends.

We were, in fact, faced with a new problem: Life had become overwhelmingly comfortable. Everything fitted in too easily for us to be able to continue to enjoy it. Like Adam and Eve in Milton's Paradise, we could have lain beneath flowery bowers all day long and done little else. But our Puritanical biases were too strong. The week came when, while buying yet another giant tin of Nescafé, we realized that we were averaging ten guest cups a day. The time had come for a Thermidorian Reaction. We shut our baize exterior door and informed our many guests that they were no longer welcome at all times of day. The initial paralyzing effects of total freedom and total leisure began to wear off and, nibbling only the occasional lotus leaf, I began to read in earnest. For the first time in my life I began to work in total freedom. No marks to reward and chastise me. I was my own master, in the pay of no man. I realized the degree to which Yale had resembled a job, how much it had fit into the American pattern of effort and reward. There I had been a worker, my pay no less real for being symbolic. Here I did what I wanted because I wanted to.

* * *

My day was not determined by any prearranged schedule. If I wanted to prepare for my supervision, I did so. I read the books that I had always wanted to read and had always put off. I read more of England's classic novels, as well as the political writings that were the basis of Fabian socialism, a creed that I felt totally at home with. The new books that tempted me succeeded in seducing me, and not only could I read them, I could persuade others to read them and could discuss them with my supervisor. This was a time of great intellectual fervor in England, and we all found ourselves swept up by the new theories of Richard Hoggart and Raymond Williams as well as those of the contributors to the exciting *Universities and Left Review*, later the *New Left Review*, that were coming from Oxford. I realized only later what this meant in terms of building an intellectual life. We were all of us free—we could all have the time. Even the dons were not tied so closely to their research and publishing that they could not join us.

At the end of my first year, I had been invited to be the editor of the leading University magazine, *Granta*. I was the first American ever offered this task and excitedly asked two of my compatriots as well as two English friends to join me. Although working in New York, I spent the summer of 1958 preparing meticulous plans and writing endless letters, and, on NAL's time, planning *Granta*'s monthly numbers. By the time September came, I had a clear idea: Each issue would center on a given theme, such as the media, utopia, or new fiction. The magazine had been around for more than one hundred years and had enough assured advertising that we did not have to worry about paying for the thousand or so issues we printed every month. I notice now that the biggest ads were proposing jobs for the RAF, with only a few, much humbler ads from the teachers' union and the nationalized Coal Board.

As for writers, though, we hardly lacked for local talent. A number of the authors we published in *Granta*, such as Margaret Drabble and Michael Frayn, would go on to become important figures in the literary world, along with journalists such as David Frost, David Leitch, and Brian Lapping. (The British media were beginning their long transformation, and this first stage involved hiring younger and younger people. Little did we guess how far this would go and how awful the British popular press would become. Tabloids such as the *Daily Mirror* actually covered the news adequately, and journalism seemed an honorable career in those pre-Murdoch days.)

There were also those engaged in politics, including many of the dons, with whom I could discuss Labour policy as an equal and who readily agreed to write for a magazine whose politics were now very clear. We were able to get articles worthy of any national paper by people such as the architectural critic Rayner Banham, the sociologist Robin Morris, and the economist Richard Layard. Indeed, we found that some of the grown-up magazines to which we sent our courtesy copies asked to reprint our articles, Jonathan Spence's article on E. M. Forster became a cover story for the *New Republic* well before Spence decided that sinology would be his life's work. Our one failure came when we idealistically turned over the magazine to some of the school's few

African students for a special issue on Africa, which failed to attract any attention—not too surprising, I suppose, in a Cambridge that had hardly any students from Ireland, let alone from the rest of the commonwealth.

We worked on a basis of equality—discussing, criticizing, asking for revisions. Writers and audience were understood to form a cohesive community, not just stratified segments. Class-ridden as Cambridge was, it had its own homogeneity. The faculty read the magazines not just in a polite attempt to keep up with undergraduate thinking, but because they were interested; just as other dons were deeply involved in the dramatic or political or other sides of the university. Cambridge as a whole expressed itself in these activities, and generally the nation was interested: the London critics would come up for the plays, and Members of Parliament referred to our articles. What mattered was the fruit of our united effort; in a way, this was what the university was supposed to be doing.

The core of the relationship with the faculty was far more than academic in the traditional sense. During my second year, I discovered the degree to which the nature of the supervisions could be altered. I had come to know enough about the faculty to find the men with whom I wished to study and to get their permission to do so. They were quite willing to bypass the formal curriculum, realizing far better than I that with a couple of months of concentrated work before the finals, I could make up the work that I had missed and still get the coveted "first" degree. The supervision system was flexible enough to become what I had hoped: a fortnightly discussion on the reading I'd just completed, guidance, disagreement, reading lists, a sympathetic supervision in the literal sense of the word. I learned more that year than I had in all my time as an undergraduate in the United States or would in graduate school.

The contact with dons extended beyond their participation in our interests; we were drawn into their lives. It was no longer a question of being formally proffered a glass of sherry at the end of the supervision. Dons would drop in unexpectedly at the end of the day, or very late in the evening if they were stuck with the job of being the tutor in residence that night, and talk about whatever was on their minds—the latest intramural battles, the chance of getting a measure passed by the university senate, the Labour Party's reaction to proposals made by a faculty group, the low or high caliber of college applicants that year. Our college had just elected a new master and the place was alive with all the changes that would follow: New college groups were being started, the level of qualifications for first-year students was being drastically raised, the general tone of the college was becoming more enlightened. A statue by Barbara Hepworth had been placed in the college garden, and the college football team at its drunkest had not dared challenge the new mood. Clare, which had been known for its athletes but not for its intellectual accomplishments, was beginning the transformation that would, in time, make it one of the top academic centers of the university.

Were we Americans an exception? Did the faculty come to us because we were outsiders—freer, perhaps more talkative, certainly better endowed with sherry? I ask the question only now because it seems an obvious one, and yet it never occurred to us then. Similar discussions were taking place throughout the university. Students visited faculty homes, and faculty students', in a way that had been undreamt of at Yale. The dinners and lunches were not the exceptions, the hearty effort of the exceptional faculty member, the occasional open house of chaplain or professor. Rather, this was the normal social life of a natural community. The faculty formed friendships with students as easily as among themselves. Of my old and good friends from Cambridge, I probably number more dons than contemporaries.

This is all the more striking when you consider the formal relationship that the university had established. We, the students, were *in statu pupillari*. They, the faculty, were *in loco parentis* and took this seriously. I remember one don telling me of being awakened in the middle of the night by a student who wanted a speck of dust removed from his eye—and he removed it, without complaining afterward. We had to apply to our tutors for permission to go beyond the city limits or, occasionally, to stay out overnight. Though he had become a good friend, my tutor still had to require me to stay after term when I once exceeded the small number of overnights I had been allotted.

In an ironic way, normal human ties had supplanted the traditional, archaic ones that were supposed to hold the university together. We were surrounded by medieval bylaws. Gowns had to be worn to all lectures, supervisions, and official functions—presumably so that mischievous undergraduates could be easily descried by university officials in case of riots or street brawls. I suppose that at heart most of us enjoyed this remnant of sumptuary legislation, though class differences in style would have largely sufficed to tell the authorities whether they were dealing with disturbers of the peace from town or gown. The latest college gate-closings were at midnight, presumably to make sure that students stayed in and studied, but in a country that was used to having its pubs, subways, and everything else close well before then, even this seemed superfluous.

We weren't, of course, so philosophic about these regulations when subjected to them, and we used to complain bitterly. To be sure, undergraduates had once been in their early teens and largely wealthy. There no longer existed any excuse for having two dons a year assigned to street patrols to make sure that under-graduates wore gowns, no matter how much they might enjoy their God-given opportunity to flirt with every girl who felt that a gown marred her party dress. Nor did the university need to spend more on maid service (two assigned to each of our rooms, plus a man for the heavier work) that was ever spent on its hope-less libraries. The number of new books was far smaller than what had been available at Yale, but then, the libraries closed so early in the day that this hardly mattered.

There were many such archaic follies, and though we were barely affected, we complained and were listened to. (I remember how Yale officials would avoid any undergraduate inquiry about administration policies, lying themselves blue in the face when questioned about such touchy matters as athletic scholarships or religious quotas.) At Cambridge, our right to question the status quo was never challenged. We were outsiders and our proposals must often have seemed ridiculous. But we were citizens of this particular community, and as such we had certain rights. Apart from this, I suspect that many of those to whom we spoke agreed with some of what we said. The individual regulations were anachronistic; to a degree, all of Oxford and Cambridge were. This helped to make the universities sacrosanct, safe as English eccentrics are safe. A few reforms might endanger the whole

structure. A guide at Versailles once explained to me the extraor-
dinary vigilance with which the guards watched the gilt wallpaper
that had just been restored at great expense. One rip had
appeared in the previous paper, and within a day the walls had
been torn bare. Cambridge was just such a gilt showcase—it could
be torn down with equal ease.

* * *

When I left Cambridge in the summer of 1959, I felt sure that
change would soon come. Cambridge and Oxford, after all, lived
at the expense of the rest of the universities. They received the
nation's best students, an unfair share of the relatively small number of youngsters who were allowed into higher education.
Parliament lavished funds on the ancient universities—funds that
until then had been given only grudgingly elsewhere. New universities were at last being planned. Public opinion demanded a
change; the Cambridge I had known was clearly threatened.

Yet this initial storm passed. Many of the new campuses were
built, and for a brief while some of them, like Sussex, challenged
the appeal of Oxbridge. But this was no real danger and the effect
on Cambridge could be discerned only with difficulty.

For years afterward my work brought me to England annually, and at the end of each visit I found myself going back to
Cambridge to visit old friends, dons, and students who have stayed
on to become dons. Each time the train approached that endless
platform I felt again the excitement of my first arrival, and for a
few days I would plunge again into Cambridge's unchanged calm
and beauty. True, the undergraduates seemed younger each year,

but for once that hardly mattered. Cambridge felt as it had before; the town, the college, the gardens had hardly altered; my contemporaries seemed much the same; I could still sense the otherness of the place and fall back into a nearly forgotten pace. I never felt like a tourist, though I could understand the thousands who drove up for the weekend; for Cambridge represents a kind of national preserve, a monument that has affected the lives of many more than just its former students. London, for instance, is dotted with minuscule copies of this academic calm. The Inns of Court, just off Fleet Street, suddenly open to the same sense of peace, and I can well understand the wealthy bachelors who sought to build an Oxbridge courtyard of their very own, in the famous Albany Apartments at the very center of London.

Going to Cambridge had been a kind of inoculation against the worst of the viruses that infected the outside world. It was well known that students found reality hard to take after leaving, and the last months at Cambridge were filled with a premature nostalgia, as people girded themselves against what was to come. After I returned to New York and was leading the life of a graduate student at Columbia that Fall, the contrast seemed almost unbelievable. Columbia was filled with anxiety and bitterness. The faculty made a point of refusing contact with the students; a real class warfare permeated the air, and one could feel the tension that finally broke out on the campus in the battles of the sixties. I had come to realize what a university was meant to be, how much more than students, teachers, and courses.

I hoped at the time that Britain would be willing to continue to pay the high price of Oxbridge because it understood how valuable the investment is, down to each of the lush flowers that decorate Clare's garden for just a few days. Oxbridge represents something that can be evaluated by every Parliament, and each time, both parties have found something there that they deeply believe in.

In its own way, Cambridge had offered both Tories and Socialists an environment in which to educate their future leaders, an environment providing an experience that neither could have without the other's consent. Within an increasingly egalitarian society, Oxford and Cambridge together composed a state endowed training school for the present and future aristocrats of the realm. Within truly noble physical surroundings students were trained at a leisurely pace that would arm them against accepting the frantic tempo of the industrial world that awaited them outside. The very best students of each generation, scientist and humanist, male and female, rich and poor, would come to know one another and form the basis of a homogeneous leadership group. The sons of the rich would be trained in a way that few of their parents could still afford. The sons of the poor would be given a taste of a standard of life that would do more to draw them away from their background than any other experience that I can imagine.

As usual, the socialists got somewhat less from the bargain, but it was still considerable. They gained a university that was then free from the taint of contemporary industrial capitalism, a taste of a society in which there was no profit motive, no productivity, no "publish or perish." Cambridge would have found the thought too incredible even to laugh at that Yale students spent countless hours competing to run the student laundry, as they did in my time, or that the editors of student publications earned thousands of dollars, but barely participated in anything else that the university offered. At Yale, all of us on scholarship spent fourteen hours each week working, washing dishes the first year, doing other jobs later. To be sure, the university did save money in this way, but far more important was the obeisance paid to puritanical doctrine. Work was necessary and would efface the stigma of poverty. Most important of all, students had to learn that you never got something for nothing. Of course one did, but the myth worked. I felt in my years at Yale that I was somehow earning my way through college; that I owed a debt, and that my job was in some way to repay it.

The whole point of Cambridge then was how much you got for nothing. No one could have really afforded its luxuries—not just the physical surroundings, but the encouragement to live a different life, to discover an altogether unknown style of life. With this first taste of leisure came that most subversive of all questions: Why work? The question had never occurred to me until Cambridge, just as it had never occurred to me that a student's room could have more than two chairs, let alone that it might contain seven. Of course, there had been comfort at Yale. The fraternities exuded an old leathery comfort, and the secret societies were said to be full of an odd watery comfort. They coexisted, just as a brothel can coexist with a strict Protestant chapel. That was the other point of Cambridge, the unity of one's existence. In a way that I had never known, my life was no longer divided or alienated. Work came from leisure, discipline from freedom; the odd paradoxes of Hegel seemed to come to life before my eyes.

This was as true of the faculty as it was of the students. For once I dealt with intellectuals, whatever their beliefs, who represented independence and the power that comes only from free-dom. Economists, critics, and historians were equally freed from the academic marketplace. We all lived on the same independent income. There was no reliance on grants or foundations or the government. The faculty could advise the government without belonging to it. They could argue, cajole, and disagree without fear of loyalty checks or oaths or what would be said about them in the RAND Corporation or the CIA. Their ivory tower was a bastion, not a refuge. Cambridge dons could go off and write constitutions for Tanganyika (and be loyal to Tanganyika, not to some Center for International Studies). They could plan development schemes for Guiana or tax reforms for Ghana. The plans might work or they might not, the men who offered them could work with government or opposition or not. They were free, knowing that their common interest in the university bound them tightly to their strongest academic opponents. It was not just that they had tenure—their world had tenure.

So the last lesson that Cambridge taught me was what real pluralism was about—the ways in which free men can really live and the alternatives they can develop. During my last year at Yale, the undergraduates and faculty had been caught up in a vast debate on whether or not the university should be a microcosm of society. The ayes were in the vast majority. With every year that has passed, our universities have increasingly resembled our society, embodying its values and training the cadres that it needed to continue. In the sixties, at least, from Berkeley on, students rebelled, realizing that they were being robbed, that they were not going to a real university, whatever that might be. Their instincts have been sound, but as we knew at Yale, you cannot discover the real simply by knowing the unreal. Real universities are not what we have been building. Once you know, it's easy to tell. Real universities subvert, they corrupt, they are dangerous things to have around, and what's more, they can be very expensive. Yet how much greater the danger—and expense—of creating a society in which no one at all knows what it's like to be truly free.

Just about all of my assumptions coming out of Cambridge proved to be wrong, and Oxbridge—that is, the academic world centered on the communities of Cambridge and Oxford—would be totally transformed by the joint efforts of Margaret Thatcher and Tony Blair. But that is for a later part of this narrative. I did feel transformed by the Cambridge experience in a number of ways: I had found an intellectual and social milieu in which I was completely comfortable; I no longer felt marginalized and combative as I had at Yale; I became a complete Anglophile and made of England my alternate country.

It may have been partly the refugee anxiety of needing another safe haven in case the first failed—the need for the folding bicycle I had felt as a child—the McCarthy period having left many of us unsure about our future in America. A number of academics, filmmakers, and others had actually found refuge in England, including some distinguished professors at Oxbridge, such as Moses Finley, the great classicist who became an important part of English intellectual life.

Intellectually, Cambridge had given me the freedom I'd never had and taught me much more than I had expected. I remember rereading Tocqueville on the French Revolution for the nth time with my supervisor, the historian Jack Gallagher, and realizing that while at Cambridge I had finally learned to read. Previously, I had read for content or for a homework assignment. But now I was understanding both the author's intentions and the questions they raised. I felt I could place the book in context in a new way, that I could see how others would have read it at the time. In other words, I was beginning to read as an historian.

In the social realm, I found a group of friends with whom I would remain close for the rest of my life. It was incredibly easy to meet people, and the natives couldn't have been friendlier. In the first weeks, every group organized meetings at which you could meet those who shared your interests. Cambridge had always had the pick of the country's brightest students. It was a case of Mark Twain's dictum, "Put all your eggs in one basket, then watch that basket." But in the late fifties it was filled with a brilliant new generation that would soon have a major impact on British intellectual and cultural life. There was a group of very funny young actors—including Jonathan Miller, Peter Cook, Eleanor Bron, and John Bird—who would create a new style of English wit in revues such as *Beyond the Fringe* and *The Second City.* I became close to many of them, such as Miller and Michael Frayn, who were then starting out. (In time, I would publish both of them.)

I had also been invited to join a discussion group called the Apostles, which later became infamous for the large number of Soviet spies that it had nurtured (such as Anthony Blunt, the famous art historian). Although it was originally a very secret and elitist group, it had been at the center of Cambridge intellectual life for many decades and was much more open by the time I joined—although the Sunday-night gatherings in the grand

King's College room of E. M. Forster were something you weren't supposed to boast about. Forster would sometimes join us, and he'd leave us a bottle of sherry when he couldn't. It was there that I met the historian Eric Hobsbawm, many of whose books I would publish, and Amartya Sen, who would later be a Nobel laureate in economics. Once a year, we would gather in London for a dinner at which some of the older members, such as Leonard Woolf, would show up, making us feel linked to the early Bloomsbury culture that he, Forster, and their fellow Apostles represented.

So I found myself in the empyrean heights of English culture, a much headier place than the relatively provincial scene at Yale. Oxbridge was very much a bridge into English intellectual life, and it would have been easy to go from there into a British publishing or an academic career. Indeed, there were opportunities even before I had left the university: I was asked if I would stay on and edit the *Cambridge Review*, the university's weekly, and refused primarily because I felt I needed to return to New York and help support my mother, both financially and emotionally. I was also offered other jobs in English publishing that I was very tempted to accept.

Also, making it the more difficult to leave was my Cambridge girlfriend.

* * *

Maria Elena de la Iglesia, as her name suggests, was not purely English. Her parents had fled to Britain at the end of the Spanish Civil War, her father having been one of the leading staff officers in the Republican army command. He had to flee the country after the fall of Madrid in 1939, and he settled, improbably, in Dartington as a geography teacher. Dartington was a utopian community created with the money of an American millionaire, Dorothy Whitney Straight, and her English husband Leonard Elmhirst, a follower of Rabindranath Tagore. They wanted to help develop the depressed English rural life in South Devon. (Odd that Tagore should appear twice in these pages, in such totally different contexts.) Maria Elena was three years old at the time, and she grew up happily in the midst of this progressive community and its experimental school, which had also invited many European artists fleeing from Hitler. By the time she arrived at Cambridge, she seemed very English, though like myself she had ties both to her original background and her new British life.

This affinity did not seem to us to be a major reason for our coming together, but it must have been the case at some level or other. She was understandably reluctant to leave her family and the country in which she had grown up. I assured her that if moving to New York didn't work out, we could move back to England, where I was sure that I could find a job as easily as in New York, and I was by then enough of an Anglophile to feel at home there.

Having received a British MA, and feeling that a PhD might be helpful, I thought I could try to continue an academic career, and so, once back in New York in late 1959, I enrolled in graduate school at Columbia. But to pay for it all and to help my mother, I took a job at the paperback firm of the New American Library, and attended Columbia late afternoons and at night.

My time at NAL proved to be a fruitful apprenticeship in publishing. NAL was the American successor to Britain's Penguin

Books and shared with it the mission of publishing serious books of literature and nonfiction. Its motto was "Good Reading for the Millions." I had read many of their books as a youngster, and working there suggested to me that books could be an alternative way of reaching a mass audience with new ideas. It could also be a different way of being involved in politics.

Partly because Cambridge had been so ideal, Columbia was worse than anything I could have imagined. Far from being a continuation of my English experience, it was a total contrast to it. Columbia was a huge assembly line that managed to crush most of its products as they were processed. For financial reasons, the university took in many more students than were qualified, then dealt with this by holding large lectures and seminars that were basically cramming sessions for the future exams. (When Columbia students rebelled a decade later, I sympathized completely with their grievances. Their slogan "Do not fold, spindle, or mutilate," adopted from the then-current IBM computer cards, was a very accurate description of what was happening to them.)

Working what were, in effect, two full-time jobs, however, did not leave me much time for politics. I kept up my links with England and the Labour Party by writing a series of articles for *Socialist Commentary*, a monthly magazine at the right of the Labour Party and one which, I later came to suspect, might have benefited from American largesse. My articles from New York were well to the left of the *Socialist Commentary*'s editorial line—I endlessly criticized John F. Kennedy and his conservative policies, both domestic and foreign. Kennedy was far too Cold War-ish, and too happy to subsume domestic agendas to an aggressive foreign policy, for my taste. Though he was then very popular in both the U.S. and England, it seemed to me that Kennedy had abandoned all of the Democrats' domestic reforms and kept the worst of the Republicans' foreign policy plans, such as the invasion of Cuba and the war in Vietnam.

By the time I started at Columbia, I had begun to wonder whether there was any sense in continuing in the adult world what I had done in SLID/SDS. Would we be able to discover any allies at a time when the Left was debating the end of ideology and the beneficial effects of automation on all our lives? We had realized that there would be no help from the tradition of the twenties and thirties. Many left-wing intellectuals had been marked by the fear of the McCarthy years. And while the unions still gave their tiny contributions to the LID, these were an homage to times long past, when Industrial Democracy was a major rallying point, a euphemism for more worker's control of the workplace.

In spite of these doubts, I decided to try to see whether the LID might be made over into something more viable, something closer to the Fabian Society that I had come to know while in England. I began a long correspondence with Shirley Williams, then Secretary of the Fabians (before she left to found the centrist Social Democrats), and proposed all sorts of joint ventures. Might we distribute Fabian material in the U.S.? Could we consider a joint magazine? I threw idea after idea out across the ocean, but the results were slim. I offered to head the LID publications committee and turned to Richard Titmuss and others I'd admired to see if we could publish their articles or pamphlets in the U.S. Here, at least, I managed to make slight progress. But in retrospect it's clear that I was trying to find a way to publish much-needed ideas in the U.S. as much as to revive the LID. And as I toiled at the New American Library by day, working on paper-backs that would reach tens or even hundreds of thousands, my attempts to import two hundred copies of a Fabian pamphlet seemed modest indeed.

Beyond these fledgling attempts at publishing, I began look-ing into what could be done about finding a new director for the LID who could reverse the years of decline. We tried various can-didates and for a while thought we had succeeded in persuading the journalist Sidney Hertzberg (father of the current *New Yorker* writer Hendrik Hertzberg) to take the helm. For a brief while, things looked up. The LID's letterhead was redesigned, and var-ious committees were established. It looked at last as if we might succeed. But Hertzberg soon decided that the difficulties were overwhelming and resigned, with no ready successor. A few peo-ple suggested my name but I did not want to plunge further into this quagmire. By early 1961, I had given up all hope and resigned as well, suggesting to the LID that the time had come to close up shop.

* * *

Since returning from Cambridge I had hoped I might play a new role. I had been asked by a group at the Rensselaer Polytechnic Institute—a college in Troy, New York—if I would be willing to engage William F. Buckley, Jr. in a public debate. Buckley was at the height of his fame then, having written not only his denunci-ation of Yale but a defense of Joe McCarthy, *McCarthy and His Enemies*. I was chosen because I'd been head of SLID/SDS, but I was basically an unknown as far as the wider world was concerned; someone there must have thought it would be interesting to have these two Yale alumni who were at such opposite ends of the spectrum meet for the first time.

I prepared meticulously for the debate, reading Buckley's published works and making careful note of his viewpoints and arguments, until finally I felt ready to meet them head-on. Buckley was, as always, suave and debonair. I felt more awkward, wearing a hand-me-down, unfashionable double-breasted suit. Yet when we met onstage, I noticed that he seemed strangely nervous. Presumably, losing the debate to me in front of the several hundred people in the vast RPI auditorium would have been humiliating. Accordingly, he focused on making his debating points rather than sticking to his old viewpoints. Buckley's main argument—in Troy, New York, of all places—was that there was no poverty in the United States. I had a hard time persuading the middle-class audience that poverty was still a major factor in our collective lives.[21] Meanwhile, all my notes were in vain, since Buckley was quick to abandon his positions whenever necessary. I tried to point out these tactics to the audience, but the debate ended in an ambiguous draw.

But this was an exceptional occasion. There were very few further opportunities to speak or to debate, except for an occasional talk on WEVD, New York's primarily Yiddish-language, Social-Democratic radio station. Its call letters were the initials of

---

[21] SLID had recently published a very effective pamphlet on income distribution by Gaby Kolko, then, briefly, our field secretary. In time, his research would influence Michael Harrington, whose *The Other America* became a major force in the sixties to the point of influencing Lyndon Johnson's War on Poverty.

Eugene V. Debs, the heroic Socialist presidential candidate. Heywood Broun, the radical thirties journalist, had a weekly program. (One of the announcers once recalled to me that Broun had often been too drunk to do his broadcast. "There's a guy who listens to me on East Tenth Street," he would inform the station. "Could you call him and say I'm sick?")

As for my organizational involvements, I felt too old to act as a would-be SDS member, but I was willing to tour some of the campuses to see if we could organize new chapters. I enjoyed going around the East Coast, and found myself trying to form a group at Harvard with Al Haber, the new SDS president. It was clear that the political situation in the colleges was very different from what it had been a few years before, and I felt hopeful about what our young successors would be able to accomplish.

But in the adult world, things were still very different. Though I occasionally represented the adult LID at various meetings, the results was hardly encouraging. The most indicative event occurred when we were faced by the Cuban missile crisis in 1962. Kennedy was playing an extremely dangerous confrontational game and people were all scared stiff. It really looked as if a nuclear conflict might break out, and we didn't even realize at that point that local Soviet commanders in Cuba had been given the authority to act. Everyone was biting their fingernails, and even though opposition to our foreign policy was still very feeble at that time, a number of liberal organizations got together to call a combined meeting of all their staffs to see what kind of protest could be organized. More than one hundred of us, representing a wide range of political and religious groups, filled a conference room of the Carnegie building (the same room, in fact, that had housed our CIA-sponsored youth meetings). Early on, Norman Thomas rose to speak. Though he was well along in years, his strong preacher's voice still resonated and he denounced the folly of Kennedy's actions. But the next speaker rose, not to continue his attack, but to pay homage to Thomas. After that, the others felt they had to recollect when they had first met Thomas, how much he had meant to them, what a grand old man he was. . . the debate on Cuba stopped before it began, swept away by this wave of left-wing nostalgia.

* * *

In the late fifties and the years to follow, many on the left abandoned the "traditional" foreign-policy and domestic issues and turned to what they felt were the newer issues. These were problems more suited to an era marked by *The End of Ideology,* Daniel Bell's very influential book that appeared in 1960. The old problems, Bell argued, had been largely solved. The new issues were centered on the effects of automation and what we would do with the resultant vast increase of leisure. They felt that society's problems would now be solved by experts and many of these intellectuals saw themselves becoming precisely these technocratic advisers. The positive side of ideology's end was that society's problems would now be solved with the help of time. Many a good person would write a book or essay on these issues before realizing how far from reality all this was, how unchanged American problems really were, how inequitable our society still was.

England's right-wing Labour MP, Richard Crossman, typified this new approach. In *The Future of Socialism,* an influential book in 1956, he wrote, "Capitalism has been reformed out of all recognition. . . . Automation can be expected steadily to resolve any remaining problems of underproduction. Looking ahead, our present rate of growth will give us a national output three times as high in fifty years." Yet within a few years, Margaret Thatcher had begun her work of destroying the welfare state, and "the bottom fifth of the workers actually became worse off compared to the rest of the workers than they had been a century earlier." [22] Britain, in recent years, could boast of 400,000 officially registered homeless. More recently, Americans faced with the devastation of Hurricane Katrina would likewise discover the degree to which extreme poverty and inequality had grown in this country in spite of the happy predictions of a half-century before.

But at that time, many on the left seemed happy to abandon their old terrain—the lot of the workers and the poor, the inequities of modern capitalism, the need for worker's control and cooperative enterprises. The fifties had taken their toll. The Left had been battered by the Cold War, smeared as pro-Soviet, suborned and assimilated. But I feel that the McCarthy period was responsible for a deeper failure of nerve. The assumption that the senator had massive popular support spread quickly and even, I think, irrationally. It would take years before studies such as Michael Rogin's 1968 book *McCarthy and the Intellectuals* would suggest the limits of McCarthy's popularity. At the time, his strength was accepted uncritically, as if it were only natural that a populist form of American fascism should develop. I suspect that

---

[22] All quotes, including Crossman: Eric Hobsbawm, *The Age of Extremes*, 268 and 308.

for many on the left, especially the Jews, the Hitlerian experience had left behind a feeling of vulnerability, the possibility that here, too, the right leader might separate us from the masses. Shorn of the certainty of working-class support, the Left shriveled, impotent, delegitimized, representing no more than an intellectual expertise looking for customers.

Many, accordingly, began to shift sides, forming the base of contemporary neoconservatism. It was as if they were saying, "If the masses were so fickle, then they did not deserve our support." Indeed, one had only to look at the new, prosperous working class, whose wages had trebled in the postwar period, to see how conservative they too had become, how bourgeois, how individualistic, how far from their old ideals. The Republicans were quick to see how important this shift had been, mining it with Nixon's Southern Strategy and Reagan's appeal to blue-collar Americans. The astute but continued use of racist appeals would help create the shift that Karl Rove and George W. Bush would exploit so successfully in this century, a story now all too well known.

Meanwhile, if mass support for the Left was no longer assured, then why bother to try to maintain the old Rooseveltian coalition? Even those on the traditional Left failed to appreciate the strength of the new movements that were developing in the late fifties and early sixties. Conditioned by years of supporting a bipartisan foreign policy, many older people were in fact suspicious of the antiwar movement and of the new student groups, typified by the SDS. Women, blacks, Greens, and others felt that they would do better by building their own movements than by joining others. The idea of a unifying party—the Socialists or even the Democrats—that was concerned with all aspects of society had been severely weakened. There was no group willing to negotiate the conflicting demands of ecologists and unions, of immigrants and black workers. Each new group found itself passionately arguing for causes that others considered threatening.

Gone too was the utopianism, the underlying hopes that had moved the Left. I became a Socialist not simply because I wanted to live in a just and equitable society, but because I realized that this would never happen if the country's basic industrial and financial structure was not changed. For us, the goal was to change these basic givens, not to create a counterculture or alternative institutions. Although, in practice, the strength of the European working class and of the African-American community was that they had created precisely such parallel cultures, Socialists believed that we nonetheless had to deal with the nitty-gritty of the mines and mills, the oil fields and the railroads. A great deal of early Socialist thinking was, in fact, devoted to making things run more efficiently, to insuring that all plants worked at capacity, rather than accepting the waste of the capitalist system. Much to our shock, however, capitalists found ways of adopting many of our ideas without abandoning their own power. We had argued that competition could be wasteful and, sure enough, the monopolists managed to eliminate it in many areas. We had argued for national planning and governmental support—the French having their own very successful five-year plans based on socializing much of the economy—and the capitalists again found ways of going along with this, as long as their profits and control were unaffected. Indeed, in Japan and in much of Southeast Asia, national planning proved immensely effective when you didn't have to deal with democratic control or equitable distribution. In America, we gradually built a system of welfare for the large corporations, and this affected every aspect of our economy, giving us all the disadvantages of Socialism and none of its virtues.

Since the nineteenth century, American liberals had argued that government regulation would preserve competition and that nationalization was simply an unnecessary ideological commitment. With globalization, however, we have seen major industries simply shutting down, abandoning plants and workers, and moving abroad, rather than risk any diminution of profit. We can certainly ask if publicly owned companies, not committed to profit maximization, might not have been a better way of maintaining national economies, as even de Gaulle argued. Or, looking at the increasing failure of America's health system, we could ask whether socialized medicine would not have been an infinitely more effective and indeed less expensive way of covering the whole of the population; or ask whether it might be better to nationalize the pharmaceutical companies, who, even though much of their research is paid for by the taxpayer, gouge the public mercilessly.

Perhaps even more important was the argument that if a democratic government did not control big business, then big business would control every aspect of government. (The Bush years have shown the extremes to which this syndrome can lead. It is no longer a question of bribing the occasional congressman to vote on a given bill. Bush's henchman Karl Rove has proved brilliantly how this can de done wholesale, how an entire government can devote itself to the specific needs of each of the industries that has paid to get it elected.)

Meanwhile, even though the sixties were upon us, they did not at first seem very different politically from the fifties. I remember visiting the spare new offices of the *New York Review of Books* just after it was launched in 1963. Its editor, Bob Silvers, had had the courage to commission an article from I. F. Stone, but he was terribly worried about the effect this would have on his readers— would people cancel their subscriptions? Assume the *Review* was pro-Communist? And so on. This, close to a decade after the Army-McCarthy hearings, which were supposed to have ended that fearful period of our life. I, too, had tried to make up for my youthful obtuseness by proposing to my bosses at Pantheon, in 1963, that we begin to publish Stone. They were afraid of doing so, and it was only many years later that I succeeded in reissuing his first book, *Underground to Palestine.* (We became friends after that and I hoped to publish his other books. But in a very American bit of irony, Stone took on a ruthlessly commercial agent who, without telling me, offered his books to other bidders.)

The relative political impasse in the U.S. showed that it made sense to turn to Europe for ideas and help—and for books. America was still suffering, intellectually as well as politically, from the combined effects of the Cold War and the McCarthy period. It would be a while before we could find again the essential work of authors who had not published during those years.

* * *

I never expected to work at Pantheon. Since my father's death, I had lost touch with the firm and, in any case, had never thought of myself as a possible successor to him—he had so many skills, so many languages. And his early death, I suppose, left me with an idealized model that I could never hope to emulate. In fact, I had never even thought of going into publishing at all. Being a librarian seemed closer to my own aspirations and possibilities. I was inspired by the role that the New York Public Library had played in my adolescence—I had spent many happy hours there and thought I would enjoy such work. There, I imagined, I could reach out to readers and be close to books that I didn't feel I could actually create, as my father had done.

So I was completely surprised when I was invited to join Pantheon as a junior editor in 1962. Pantheon, along with Knopf, had just been bought by Random House, and those running the firm felt the need to strengthen its staff. At first I worked on the manuscripts that were already in-house, but in time I began to think of books that I might be able to add to the list.

When I was given approval to go abroad to search for books, my thoughts turned first to England, then to the Continent. My Cambridge years had brought me close to the British political and intellectual scene, and I felt a part of the debates that were taking place there. I also knew that there were many in England whose ideas I shared and who were well ahead of what little debate existed in post-McCarthy America. Many English publishers were still committed to the Labour Party, and its intellectual tradition was still strong. Though the Cold War had had some effect, the British Left was already renewing itself. A new generation around the *Universities and Left Review* (later to become the *New Left Review*) had created an exciting new climate, with authors such as Richard Hoggart, Edward P. Thompson, and Raymond Williams. I had reviewed one of the first books to gather the writings of this group, *Out of Apathy*, in 1960 for the *New Republic*. (That magazine, then still very much on the American Left, allowed me to write a number of articles before it changed ownership and direction.)

Going to London for Pantheon from 1964 on, I was thrilled to meet people whom I had tried to publish at the LID, such as Richard Titmuss, and was even more excited that I could now publish their key works. I was particularly pleased to publish *The Gift Relationship*, the book in which Titmuss brilliantly used blood-donating as a metaphor for the organization of society: Blood was donated in England and Europe, but often sold in the U.S., where it was at risk of being contaminated by being bought from the desperate and the drunk, as opposed to being voluntarily given by society at large. This offered a marvelous contrast between Europe's welfare state and America's capitalist economy. In the happy days when John Leonard was editing the *New York Times Book Review*, books such as Titmuss' were given front-page reviews and listed among the year's ten most important works. (Such decisions doubtless helped to shorten Leonard's tenure at the *Times*.)

I had no trouble finding books by my idols, such as R. H. Tawney, whose Christian Socialism had greatly influenced my own thinking in the fifties. But there was also a younger generation of social scientists and political thinkers, people who had followed the exciting breakthrough of Hoggart and Williams and others who had transformed our intellectual life at Cambridge. Affiliated with the journal *Past and Present* was a group of brilliant Marxist historians such as Christopher Hill and Eric Hobsbawm, both of whose books I would publish.

I also visited older British publishers such as Victor Gollancz, who had been the center of left-wing publishing during the thirties with his *Left Book Club*. He was still very active during the postwar period, and we formed an important partnership that saw me publishing American editions of Gollancz's books, such as Edward Thompson's masterly *The Making of the English Working Class,* and Gollancz publishing UK versions of Pantheon books, such as the very first book we did together, Gunnar Myrdal's *Challenge to Affluence.* (A critique of the American economy, the book would in time influence Lyndon Johnson's plans for his War on Poverty; Myrdal was proud when he learned that the book was seen on Johnson's desk.)

Gollancz still worked in the same Covent Garden building that he had occupied in the thirties. His small office, up several flights of steps, was suitable shabby, its floor covered with the day's correspondence and manuscripts. We were very far from the sleek corporate suites of today's British publishers. (Not that Gollancz himself didn't live rather well—he would always invite me to a posh lunch at the Savoy, by far the fanciest of the meals I ever had during my annual visits.) His building's core was a huge, airy stockroom, several stories high, where buyers from the London bookstores would go to select from the current books. Once, in a corner, I found stacks of the old orange-covered *Left Book Club* editions, which they were glad to sell me for the old price. I still treasure the books by Orwell and others that I found there—rare memories of another era, which, surprisingly, no used-book dealer had bothered to corner.

* * *

As important were the younger editors at Penguin and at other British houses who shared my political views and were willing, and able, to share the publishing risks of many of our books. At that time, publishers were not under the draconian profit pressures that came with conglomerate ownership, and editors such as those at Penguin and elsewhere were able to take on books in which they believed but whose salability was far from assured. In Europe as well as in England and the U.S., publishers were accustomed to an average annual profit of 3 percent. My new bosses at Random House were happy if we didn't lose money and expected, at best, a very modest profit, which we were able to achieve. The Penguin editors carried around a little chart showing how many copies they needed to print for each of their Commonwealth branches, but the numbers were reasonable. All of us felt empowered to take risks, intellectually as well as commercially. My old hopes of international cooperation proved possible, at least in publishing, and I was able to acquire books by important writers by sharing the cost of production and advances with British publishers and, in return, giving them rights for UK editions, or vice versa.

This kind of teamwork supported some remarkable discoveries. For example, at Penguin's urging I took on the then-barely-known radical psychoanalyst R. D. Laing, as well as much of their history and politics lists. They were willing to try our new American authors, such as Noam Chomsky. Chomsky's critique of the Vietnam War had seemed to me the most telling and trenchant of all the American voices. I had foolishly waited too long before publishing books on the conflict, assuming with my old optimism that the war was such folly that it couldn't possibly continue. It soon became clear that I was all wrong, and when I read a long article about the war by Chomsky in the *New York Review of Books*, I immediately asked him if we could publish it as a book. He agreed and added some of the major essays—such as his defense of anarchist philosophy—that made the book so important, beyond its critique of the war. The result, *American Power and the New Mandarins,* proved to be the ideal attack. Chomsky's reputation as a political critic was launched internationally when Penguin took on the book as a paperback, and most of my European colleagues followed suit. Many were surprised that a philosopher known to them only as a linguist should turn out to be the keenest of critics of America's policies, as he remains to this day.

The other new author who found acceptance just about everywhere in the world was Studs Terkel. His radio-interview programs in Chicago had shown his unique ability to listen to people, a rare gift, and reading them in his station's magazine made me realize that he could be a perfect successor to Gunnar Myrdal's son Jan Myrdal, whose *Report from a Chinese Village* I had just published. I asked Terkel if he could write an American equivalent of Myrdal's work. Terkel's subsequent *Division Street, America* did for the common people of the U.S. what Myrdal had tried to do in China, and it was an immediate success. Terkel would go on to write, in many volumes, a veritable oral history of America, from the Great Depression to the present day, although I never suspected that his books would be such phenomenal successes or that our collaboration would last close to fifty years.

After Terkel's initial success I asked other writers throughout the world to follow his lead, and our village series was published widely. My idea was to do a collective portrait of everyday life that would parallel the achievement of the historians of the common people we had published—E. P. Thompson, Eric Hobsbawm, and their American counterparts, Eugene Genovese and Herbert Gutman. The last arrow in this quiver was the collection of folk-tales from all over the world that I built around the re-releases of collections of Grimm and Afanasev, books I had inherited from my father's Pantheon. We ended up with more than a dozen such volumes, which sold extremely well and gave us another aspect of this triptych reconstructing all aspects of everyday life—history, oral history, and popular culture.

As for Jan Myrdal himself, my work with him had come as a result of my political hopes in Sweden, that staunch upholder of traditional Social Democracy. I had met his father, Gunnar Myrdal, when he had given a speech in New York. Gunnar was another of my idols, the author of *An American Dilemma,* which had been the most telling analysis of America's racial problems in the forties. I had persuaded him to write *Challenge to Affluence,* a little book in which he showed how America's racial and economic inequities were linked. Gunnar's comments were rarely welcomed by the American press, who considered him a scolding Dutch uncle. Thanks to him I had endless introductions in Sweden, and I had started to travel to Stockholm every other year. Few if any American publishers had ever done this, and I found I had the pick of the country's best authors, in literature and in nonfiction. Here, too, there were many idealistic young publishers eager to collaborate, and I soon found that I had a wide range of possible partners. They joined me in commissioning American and European books and in turn I found foreign publishers for

Swedish authors who normally would not have appeared beyond their borders.[23]

France also became an obvious ally, but there the attraction went beyond politics. I found myself feeling very much at home on my annual visits there, and I discovered that I enjoyed the lunches and conversations as much as the discovery of authors. I never thought of myself as anything but a lucky American, but obviously the French saw me as very much a product of their culture. At some subconscious level, I must have enjoyed this reimmersion in French life, and I sought as many books as possible to try out in America.

I was also still naïve enough to think that I could bring to the U.S. many of the authors who had succeeded in France but were unknown on the other shore. I didn't realize that a book would be sold less on its merits than on its author's fame. French journalists like André Fontaine and Claude Julien, both editors of *Le Monde*, had written books on the Cold War and American foreign policy that I thought could find an American audience. But their names were unknown on the other side of the Atlantic and, no matter how important and timely their books were, they never reached more than a very limited audience.

The same was true with other intellectual fare. The anti-psychiatry movement was growing in France and Italy, and at Pantheon we translated a number of important books on the sub-

---

[23] As for the Myrdal family: Not only did I publish Gunnar, but I would go on to publish many books on Asia by Jan; his daughter Sissela Bok's influential books *Lying and Secrets*; and his wife Alva's *The Game of Disarmament*, about her work in the field, for which she received the Nobel Peace Prize. Gunnar *also* won a Nobel, in Economics, in 1974.

ject by noted experts such as the analysts Octave and Maud Mannoni. But in spite of their established reputations, their books had little or no influence on their American colleagues. The same was true of R. D. Laing, who was fascinated by the work of his European colleagues but whose many books that I published in the U.S. never got the slightest attention in the analytical journals, although—and perhaps *because*—he became increasingly popular with the young sixties generation.

Laing also shared my interest in the French historian Michel Foucault, whose work he helped publish in England. One of my most exciting discoveries in France had come with my finding, in a Paris bookstore, of Foucault's *History of Madness,* which I needlessly retitled *Madness and Civilization.* Here was an historian as original and exciting as those I had found in England. But Foucault's book had failed to interest any of the American university presses in the years after its publication, and when the reviews of our edition of *Madness* came out, I could see why. One major historian criticized Foucault, who had written the book while teaching in Poland, for failing to cite his archival sources. Others proved equally unimpressed. Clearly the profession was hostile to such new approaches, and it took close to a decade before we could even persuade an American university to invite Foucault to lecture, much less to assign his books.

Yet for me, simply talking with Foucault was an exciting intellectual experience. We would lunch in Paris every year and discuss his plans for his next book, an ever more exciting series that went from his history of madness to that of knowledge and power, to punishment and control, and finally to sexuality, all linked in ways that were fascinating to discover. Our conversations were like a ping-pong game in which the ball is batted with greater and greater speed. Simply talking with him made me feel much more intelligent than I was (even though my comments were basically questions). It was an experience I had only had before when talking with Noam Chomsky. Later, when American universities finally began to acknowledge Foucault's work and to invite him to lecture, we would meet in New York as well. I enjoyed introducing him to American writers and intellectuals, such as Susan Sontag, who understood his work, and I joked with Maria Elena that were we ever to publish the list of guests at these dinner parties, they would be far more interesting than any memoirs I might ever write.

But it was not only in meeting authors that I felt the adrenaline flow—there were many publishers, too, who were brilliant and exciting colleagues. I felt that people like Paul Flamand, the head of Le Seuil, François Maspero of Maspero, and Jerome Lindon of Minuit were role models who had accomplished far more than any American contemporary. Flamand, the older representative of left-wing Catholicism, had turned Seuil into the main publisher of new social thought. At Minuit, which had started out as an underground publisher during the war, Lindon not only published the French avant-garde, such as Marguerite Duras and Claude Simon (both of whose books I would eventually publish in the U.S.), but many leading social critics, such as Pierre Bourdieu and others critical of the Algerian war. Maspero represented the new generation of French radicalism, publishing books that attacked French policies in Algeria and elsewhere, books often censored and seized by a government that had never heard of the First Amendment and sought to drive Maspero out of business. He, too, took on Chomsky and many of our new history books.

Being in France also gave me a chance to hear about the new novelists, the historians and anthropologists. Many had little to do with my political agenda, but their work was clearly important and worth trying out in America. I also came to feel, perhaps unconsciously, ever closer to French culture and thought.

So I always left Paris feeling that I had had a year's worth of intellectual excitement in a week, even more than in my time in London or elsewhere. I became more of a general publisher, finding historians and social scientists who would make an impact on American thought, though primarily in the universities. In time, as other publishers found that profit pressures discouraged their taking on foreign authors, I became the American publisher of such known figures as Simone de Beauvoir and Duras. Even our colleagues at Knopf felt reluctant to carry on with Sartre, and I happily offered to replace them. Gradually Pantheon became again the obvious place for European publishers to approach, and the list grew impressively.

The pleasure of my European excursions grew as we began to have a new generation of American writers to offer in exchange. But it came about slowly. Gradually the sixties began to be marked by an intellectual as well as a political fervor. By late in the decade, we had found the new generation of historians, social scientists, literary critics, and others who were to form the university debate of the late sixties and on into the seventies. In 1968, I started a series of "anti-textbooks" that brought together the young dissidents in various fields, and we soon found that there was a whole generation of committed academics who could nourish the activists on campus as well as those involved in the civil-rights and antiwar movements.

* * *

In the spring of 1968 I had been in New York when the rebellion swept through Paris, but even several months later, during my annual visit, I could see the remains of the would-be revolution's activities. Posters were still on the walls, and even the charred remains of a car could occasionally be seen. The French had hoped that major changes would be possible in their frozen nineteenth-century structures. The rebellion had been not only about de Gaulle's policies; it had hoped to overturn the hierarchic assumptions of the French universities and professions, where those at the top took credit for all the work done by the younger staff and ruthlessly determined their futures. But in spite of the protests and the speeches, very little had actually been accomplished. Many of the gestures toward the students, such as allowing them on university boards, turned out to be more symbolic than real, although, politically, 1968 confirmed the French Left's commitment to revolution in the Third World, and its opposition to America's war in Vietnam, its backing of Castro and Ché's guerrilla forays in Latin America.

Even the usually staid and commercial Frankfurt Book Fair was caught up that year in the revolutionary excitement, and we held endless meetings, with radical publishers joining local students to hear Daniel "Danny the Red" Cohn-Bendit and others. Unfamiliar with the city, we gathered in the few places we knew: The normally quiet and affluent Frankfurt hotels gave way and allowed us to hold mass meetings in their lobbies. Hotel officials quietly receded into the background, hoping that the local students wouldn't stain their posh furniture.

With the events of 1968, publishers everywhere found themselves swept up in the new expectations for change and even revolution. My American colleagues became much more daring, and even the staid older houses, such as Harper & Row, began to publish much more radical stuff. We also found ourselves acting together, perhaps for the first time in American history. We started an organization called Publishers for Peace that took on rather symbolic acts of protest, such as walking out on Vice President Hubert Humphrey when that hapless man addressed the National Book Awards at Lincoln Center. We also organized a public rally against the Vietnam War in front of the New York Public Library. When, years later, my children persuaded me to use the Freedom of Information Act to obtain my FBI files, I found to my dismay that most of what they would send me was a handful of press clippings describing these anodyne activities. There were also a number of heavily censored memos listing my contacts with the European Left, which may have also been garnered from newspaper articles or possibly from having me tailed. Curiously, there were no photos of my trip to Cuba, though I had been very ostentatiously photographed at the Mexico City airport in 1968. I asked the local photographers who they were working for, and they naively answered, "The government." When I pressed them and asked, "Whose?" they simply smiled and shrugged their shoulders.[24]

---

[24] In spite of the State Department's many obstructions, I had managed to get to Cuba, and I found myself impressed by the social progress yet worried by something else: A new wave of censorship had swept over Cuba's books and newspapers. Though I found one historical work to translate, I encountered an unwillingness to take anything on from the U.S. On a later trip in the eighties, I found the system of censorship permanently in place and we gave up on our efforts to get any American thought onto the island.

All our catalogues reflected the era's new hopes, the new approaches. They would continue in this vein for several years, as Johnson gave way to Nixon, and as the Vietnam War continued on its tragic path. It would take a while, until the joint accession of Thatcher and Reagan, for the tide to begin to turn.

The late sixties also brought exposés of the CIA's many political and cultural activities. Since learning about the CIA's backing of our efforts at the Vienna conference I had attended as a student, I had tried, fruitlessly, to tell people of its nefarious practices. I would warn my British friends of the money behind the magazine *Encounter*, and my French colleagues about its local equivalent, *Preuves*. But no one listened to me or cared very much. Articles in the American magazine *Ramparts* and then elsewhere made the issue a public one and, for a while, Senator Frank Church's investigations as well as other protests looked as if they might be effective. But the CIA was clever enough to circumvent these limits and soon found other ways of continuing its policies. The National Endowment for Democracy would be created to continue much of what had been the CIA's overseas funding; it was theoretically aboveboard but was soon left to its activities with little if any political or journalistic supervision. A rare article in a recent *New York Times* issue described the NED's activities in Haiti, where its Republican Institute acted exactly as the CIA had in the old days, pushing the local opposition and financing thuggish groups that would together create the chaos that led to President Jean-Bertrand Aristide's ouster. It was a program very similar to what the CIA had done in Central America from Eisenhower on, but this time it was done outside the formal cover of the Agency.

More important was the funding of foreign political parties, a practice which had been rife in postwar Europe and which I had noticed in England, and which now continued apace. To give one example: We were vacationing in Spain in 1977 when, for the first time since Franco, a Socialist party was running a candidate in the parliamentary elections. I was puzzled by the huge number of posters that appeared even in the small town in which we were staying. How could the newly legalized party have such deep pockets? Later, Henry Kissinger would boast in his memoirs how the U.S. had channeled secret funds through the German Social Democratic party to influence both the Spanish and Portuguese Socialist parties. A few years later, I published a book by Willy Brandt, the German Socialist leader, and at a dinner at our house, I decided that it would be a good occasion to check the veracity of Kissinger's account. "Typical of Henry," Brandt laughed. "It was our idea, but he had taken credit for it." What presumably had started as the German Socialist's solidarity with the outlawed Spanish Socialist party (the PSOE) gradually become an effective part of American foreign policy. The Socialist Felipe Gonzáles was elected in spite of his policy of wanting Spain to join NATO, something that his party bitterly opposed. But in time, Kissinger's clever investment won out, and Gonzáles managed to get Spain to join the Atlantic Alliance in spite of his party's adamant refusal.

In the heady atmosphere of the late sixties, however, no one gave any thought to the possibility of a reactionary counterrevolution. It would take a few years to realize how powerful that kind of action would be. We were pleased with the changes that were taking place in publishing and in public opinion. For a while, into the early seventies, we felt that politics had really changed, that the opposition to the Vietnam War would succeed, that real changes would take place in America's long, tortured history of racial inequality.

The new leadership of the SDS issued their early statements, like the famous Port Huron declaration in 1962. This was in many ways inspired by our old arguments for Industrial Democracy—or worker's control, as it was restyled. But the real impetus for change would come not from the students but from the civil-rights movement. The great March on Washington took place in 1963. The sit-ins and other protests in the South galvanized the country and suddenly gave the Left what it had so badly lacked: clear goals and a broad, mass membership. The students followed, rather than led, but here was something real that would move a very broad group of Americans.

* * *

As students joined the civil-rights movement, they were introduced to a totally different America, to a reality they had only known in theory. That was in part the result of going to the South and facing harassment and arrest. When, in 1968, the action moved to the North and was focused on the students' own universities, they discovered much more than complicity in the Vietnam War. Their enemies often turned out to be their own professors and university administrators. Some of their teachers, once left-wingers themselves, would see in the students not a new version of themselves but threatening Maoists who were ready to destroy the very foundations of Western civilization. Though some of their mentors, like Herbert Marcuse, were European exiles, others saw in the students a frightening replica of what had happened in Nazi Germany. The students were certainly disrespectful, but they also seemed to their professors to be frighteningly irrational. I would meet academics who boasted of having left rebellious campuses like Yale (!) to seek safer havens—where, they boasted, they would no longer be confronted by students who disagreed with them in class.

Next to the civil-rights movement, the war itself was the most important factor. The Korean War had gone largely unnoticed in America, meeting with no opposition, covered only very partially by the media. This time the war was on every television screen, showing horrors that most Americans could never have imagined. The threat of the draft brought this home, even to those enjoying student deferments. Fear of being directly involved was a major, perhaps *the* major, reason for student opposition, and this taught a lesson to the Pentagon that it put to effective use in preparing today's wars; there is little doubt that the abolishment of the draft has been due to that sixties opposition more than to anything else.

Added to the destruction of Vietnam's villages was the destruction of our own assumptions about our democracy. Why were our experts, the famous "best and brightest," unable to control events? Why did they refuse to respond to all the democratic pressures that were supposed to work? The students, along with an increasing number of their fellow citizens, began to lose faith and turn to extra-parliamentary action: to marches, sit-ins, and other token acts of civil disobedience.

If governments could not be trusted, then why bother with the reforms that we had advocated? While we had been concerned with changing the nature of the commanding heights of the economy, as they were called, this new generation became obsessed with parallel institutions, with the counterculture, with creating their own alternative society. In a way this was more conservative, though far more practical, than our agenda had been. No one thought any more about changing the goals of government or of industry, of replacing the profit motive with long-range social planning. The students were concerned with developing their own newspapers and radio stations, even with creating their own alternative universities. Far from wanting to destroy the concept of the university (as the conservative faculty charged), they wanted to create a better and freer one. In 1968, in a sweltering Columbia auditorium, I listened with several hundred others as Edward Thompson lectured on William Blake. Thompson was glad to speak to the students, helping them show that their rebellion was not an antiintellectual one but rather one that sought to broaden the curriculum, to bring in new voices that the university had been reluctant to recognize. Gradually a new generation of graduate students and younger faculty began to change the curriculum in a way that still horrifies the Right. Pantheon's antitextbooks were widely used, but more important, the new generation of radical scholarship that they represented began to flourish. Whole new fields of study were developed: Areas such as Black history and women's studies emerged and began to proliferate. For me, an important part of the excitement of those years was reading new manuscripts in such fields and seeing them become part of the intellectual fervor of the times.

But intellectual debate exists in a very real context, and as American politics changed, we found ourselves increasingly on the defensive. The policies of Nixon and then Reagan put the Left in a situation of trying to prevent the worst abroad, rather than improve the situation at home.

Looking back, historians can trace the decline of the West, the end of the postwar boom—the "thirty glorious years," as the French called them—to the oil crisis that hurt all the Western economies. Unemployment soared and voters increasingly were willing to turn rightward to solve the problems they lived with.

But it would be inaccurate to say that we were at all aware of these long-term changes at the time. As Eric Hobsbawm writes in *The Age of Extremes,* "The history of the twenty years after 1973 is that of a world which lost its bearings and slid into instability and crisis. And yet, until the 1980s it was not clear how irretriev-ably. . . Not until the early 1990s do we find admissions that the economic problems of the present were actually worse than those of the 1930s."[25]

Life in America became dominated by a series of crises initial-ly linked more to foreign policy than to domestic issues. The Vietnam War, until its conclusion in 1975, was the center of our attention and our passions. Increasingly it dominated what we thought and what we published. It was the protests against the war

---

[25] Eric Hobsbawm, *The Age of Extremes,* 387.

that led Nixon to take increasingly illegal actions to defend not only his regime but his determination to circumvent the constitutional limits on his presidency. His opponents saw themselves fighting on both fronts, and the battle lines were more clearly drawn than at any time until the debacle of George W. Bush.

At Pantheon, as we published more and more books on Vietnam and on Nixon, I still felt that we were dealing with a temporary crisis brought on by Nixon's paranoia. Even though I was very proud of publishing Noam Chomsky's many books, my old reformist instincts kept me from completely accepting his view that it was America itself that had been transformed into an imperial fortress, one that could not be changed by demonstrations and partial reforms. But as time passed, Chomsky's analysis seemed more and more convincing. After a brief respite during the Ford and Carter administrations, we found ourselves in the disastrous throes of the Reagan years. Again, instead of publishing new ideas about where America should go, we reacted to the endless series of crises brought about by Reagan's determination to overcome the post-Vietnam syndrome, the American public's wariness of ever again finding themselves in such an imperial quagmire. Reagan began the effort slowly and farcically, with the invasion of the tiny island of Grenada, but he soon expanded it into a series of incursions into Latin America, with his ludicrous characterization of the murderous Contras as resistance fighters. Finally, there was the Iran-Contra scandal, with its array of White House buccaneers given a free hand by a president who later claimed the excuse of incipient Alzheimer's.

But outrageous as these policies were, they determined the national agenda and hence what we had to publish—again, endless books on Latin America, on the rebirth of American imperialism, and on domestic policies that sought, with varying degrees of success, to undo the legacy of the New Deal.

In England, Margaret Thatcher was even more successful in her attempts to severely limit the welfare state brought about by Labour in the postwar years. She sought to undermine the very foundations of Socialist thought, arguing famously that there was no such thing as "society." People were encouraged to think of greed as a virtue, to look out only for themselves, and to abandon unions and other structures that were based on the assumption that workers could make the most progress by acting together instead of hoping that the bosses would reward them for their individual talents and accomplishments. Public services were diminished, industries were privatized, and many of the accomplishments that had made England such an exciting and agreeable place to live were undermined. Going back to London during those years, I would gradually notice the effects of Thatcherization in the ever-filthier streets as civic budgets were slashed, and in the growing number of beggars and homeless—sights that we had assumed had disappeared from the country forever. English cultural life, meanwhile, was also changing, with, for example, the transformation of London's theatres into adjuncts of Broadway's commercialization (with the few, important exceptions of the national theatres).

Worse, as far as I was concerned, was the alteration of Britain's publishing houses. More and more of them were bought up by conglomerates that imposed drastic profit targets on the editors. Most of my contemporaries were fired, replaced by young people who, knowing no other values, had internalized the

Thatcherian goals and assumed they were the norm. Year by year, my address book became filled with the blacked-out names of good friends and collaborators, as well as of literally dozens of publishing houses, which had disappeared. Within a short period, I found I could have all my appointments in a few shiny new office buildings rather than at the many small houses I used to visit. Marvelous old publishing houses with distinguished histories were each turned into a floor—or even simply a desk—in the new conglomerate headquarters. A pathetic occasional bookshelf, filled with the works of D. H. Lawrence or George Orwell, would act as a marker—or rather as a tombstone—for what had once been a vibrant group of committed editors.

The impact on the universities was equally disastrous. Production quotas were imposed on faculties until they complained that they now spent nearly as much time filling out bureaucratic forms as they did teaching. Eventually, under Tony Blair, the concept of free tertiary education was undermined, and increasingly steep fees were imposed—theoretically on those whose families could pay, but gradually also on students who, as in America, had to borrow the money. This had the predictable and doubtless intended effect of ensuring that graduates would move to higher-paying corporate jobs in order to pay off their debts, and thus direct labor away from public service to the all-important private sector. The days when many of my Cambridge classmates were happy to become schoolteachers were well behind us. Now the City of London beckoned, and England became a center of money making money, rather than a producer of goods and ideas.

England's mass media were also transformed, with first its print media and then its television becoming relentlessly down-market and politically extreme, even vicious. Previously decent and informative tabloids turned to scandal, pinups, and mostly reactionary politics. The transition was led by Rupert Murdoch, whose News Corp. was able to gain control of some of the country's leading newspapers, including its most popular tabloid, the *Sun*, and the once-crucial voice of the establishment, the *Times* of London, the contents and format of which were transformed. The effect of Murdoch on the nation's politics and morals were widespread, and Blair soon found that he had to make deals with Murdoch to retain his support. Murdoch papers had headlined the defeat of Labour in the election before Blair's ultimate victory in a famous, fraudulently populist headline, IT'S US WOT BEAT HIM. Upon finally being elected, Blair's immediate response was to fly to Italy and lobby Italian Prime Minister Silvio Berlusconi to allow Murdoch's SKY TV access to Italy's airwaves. What seemed at first merely craven opportunism later proved to be a new and lasting alliance when Blair, Berlusconi, and Murdoch all worked together to support George W. Bush's Iraq policies. (Murdoch would be quoted as saying at the time of the Iraqi invasion, "We can not retreat now or we will abandon the Middle East to Saddam. Bush is acting in a very moral fashion.... The best thing that could happen to the world economy would be oil at twenty dollars a barrel. That would be better than any tax cut in any country."[26] As we know, oil recently reached eighty dollars a barrel.)

We should have seen, in the effect of Murdoch on the popular press in Britain and Australia, what the dangers in America

---

[26] *Bulletin* magazine (Australia), February 2003.

would be. Soon enough, Murdoch was able to use his political influence in the United States to get an exemption from the Federal Communications Commission regulation stipulating that no single company could own both a TV station and a newspaper in the same city. (According to an early biography, Murdoch once offered Jimmy Carter the support of the traditionally Democratic *New York Post* if Carter would agree to his plans to buy an airline as well.[27]) Soon, Murdoch's leading American outlets, the *New York Post* and Fox television, would become powerful purveyors of an extreme right-wing populism unseen in America since the worst days of the Hearst press.

It is ironic that those of us in the book business, despite our preoccupation with the political dangers surrounding us, failed to see how soon this phenomenon would be replicated in our very own domain.

* * *

The Random House that had bought Pantheon in 1961 was still very much in the classic mode of American publishing. Bennett Cerf and Donald Klopfer had owned the firm since its inception and did with it as they pleased. It was still a relatively small house, primarily publishing popular American writing, with a list that included some of the major figures in American literature, such as William Faulkner, John O'Hara and James Michener. Bob Haas, who had joined the company in 1936, had brought with him some

---

[27] Thomas Kiernan, *Citizen Murdoch* (New York: Dodd Mead, 1986).

noted European authors, such as Isak Dinesen and André Malraux. But it was the merger with Knopf in 1960 that had brought to the firm the most distinguished of the American lists. Adding Pantheon gave the group an equally distinguished list of European titles, including the recently very successful *Doctor Zhivago* and Giuseppe di Lampedusa's *The Leopard.* It also brought to Random a younger generation of editors that could continue the kind of international publishing for which Knopf had been known. There was no one at Knopf who had links to this area and who shared the interests of Blanche and Alfred Knopf, who had run the firm from the beginning, and they considered me a possible successor. Blanche was very cordial, and she invited me to lunches where I watched appalled as this already skeletal woman toyed with a lettuce leaf and tried indirectly to find out whether I might be interested in the famously dangerous post of being their dauphin (a job that never seemed to last more than a few years). Once it was clear that my own interest was in continuing and preserving what my father had helped to create at Pantheon, Bennett and Donald were happy to see what we could do there instead.

It's an aspect of American law that is too little discussed, but it is clear that our system is geared against the family firm and toward the corporation. The latter entity is eternal; families are doomed to die off, and Alfred Knopf had sold his firm to avoid the inheritance taxes that would have been inevitable otherwise. The same dilemma faced Cerf and the others a few years later, when they felt constrained to sell their newly expanded group to the electronics giant RCA. In his memoirs, *At Random,* Cerf says that he assumed he could continue to publish the books they liked. This attitude proved to be both naïve and optimistic about corporate ownership, but it was very common among publishers at that time.

When RCA took over, it brought with it the whole panoply of corporate assumptions: Profits were expected to increase with every quarter, growth with every year. Each of Random's imprints—each segment of the firm—would become a profit center, judged by its ability to produce the required results. Most importantly, the very purpose of the firm was transformed: Money was now the sole object. Random mattered not for the books it published, but for the ways in which it could fit into the greater corporate structure.

RCA expected Random's textbooks, known widely in publishing as the firm's weakest aspect, to be linked to RCA's new "teaching machines"—early approximations of computers—to produce Wall Street's new buzzword, synergy. Within a few years, teaching machines would prove too clunky and would be short-lived. In any case, Random's inadequate textbooks would be limited by antitrust legislation from feeding the teaching machines, and thus the company was spared the humiliation of publicly revealing its weaknesses.

But while all of this led to RCA's getting rid of Random within just a few years (as other electronics behemoths did with their eagerly acquired publishing houses), the structures it imposed upon Random remained in place. Bob Bernstein, Bennett's successor, had protected us as much as he could from RCA's irrational expectations, but he had been forced to alter the old Random. I remember walking to work with Bob through Central Park, as we often did, and hearing from him that Pantheon would now be a profit center. I was far from clear as to what that would mean, but I discovered all too soon how disastrous it would be. As an independent firm, Pantheon had survived due to the profits made from all of its several tiny departments. For example, the very successful children's-book list helped carry the firm before it hit the jackpot with huge bestsellers such as *Doctor Zhivago*. A number of books were used in college courses, including Albert Camus' *L'Etranger*, as well as other titles that my father had originally published.

When I had started at Pantheon, coming straight from my experience at NAL, my first move was to start our own paperback line, which was very successful. It was made up of titles we had published first in hardcover, such as *The Tin Drum* by Günter Grass, and *Gift from the Sea*, Anne Morrow Lindbergh's huge inspirational bestseller. The new structure began stripping us of all these assets. The children's list was the first to go, made to merge with Knopf's. Our paperbacks became part of Vintage, and so on. The battle to retain the profits from these paperbacks would last until I left, but it would prove fatal to others. Ann Godoff, the very able head of the Random House trade list, would be ignominiously fired a few years later because her profits were deemed to be inadequate. If she had been credited with the paperback revenues that were rightfully hers, she would have been everything that the Bertelsmann Corporation, the new owners of Random House, could have hoped for.

Thus, the new corporate standards proved to be dangerous, indeed often fatal, to intelligent publishing. Books that might take years to write did not fit neatly into a pattern of increasing quarterly profits. Bernstein did his best to explain this to RCA, but throughout the publishing business one could see more and more irrational decisions being made to please new conglomerate owners: Christmas books would be published in August to fill out that quarter's sales projections, and so on. Growth, which was difficult to achieve by simply publishing books, was therefore often accomplished by buying other firms, no matter how inappropriate. Most important, the firm's profits were not only expected to grow, but eventually to approximate profits made by other holdings, including much more profitable divisions in film, television, and the press. In the U.S. and in Europe, publishing as a whole had averaged a 3-to-4-percent annual profit throughout the century. Wall Street was looking for profits in the range of 10 to 20 percent. Clearly the twain could not meet, even with the hoped-for synergy, and the first wave of mergers in the publishing industry ended rapidly.

When Random House was dumped by RCA in 1980, everyone at the firm was delighted that it was then bought by S. I. Newhouse and his media conglomerate, Condé Nast. Newhouse arrived promising us all that he believed in what we all were publishing and would change nothing at all in our output or structure. Known for his fabulous collection of modern art and his willingness to subsidize his wife's own small, independent program of books in architectural history, Newhouse seemed at first the very model of an enlightened capitalist. None of us thought to look into what his policies had been elsewhere, so relieved were we to be freed from RCA's grip.

But we soon discovered that the Condé Nast conglomerate expected even greater profits from us, and would soon transform Random House. Newhouse—Si, as he was called—quickly sold off Random's school and college divisions and bought instead the down-market firm of Crown, which proved to be worth far less than he had paid for it. The loss of the college division made it far harder for Knopf and Pantheon to sell our own books to colleges.

At this point, I should have realized that Pantheon could not survive long. Though we had never lost any money for Random, as Bob Bernstein often assured me, we were clearly not going to maximize Newhouse's profits, and we would soon share the fate that awaited another of his new holdings, the *New Yorker* magazine. As part of Newhouse's master plan, Bernstein was fired and replaced by an incompetent former banker named Alberto Vitale, who boasted to all and sundry that he was far too busy ever to read a book. His office was hygienically free of these offensive, dust-gathering objects and featured only a photograph of his yacht. Spared the onerous task of reading, Vitale instead promised Newhouse that his managerial skills would produce vast new profits. It would take only a few years for Newhouse to discover that while Vitale would succeed in pushing the firm further down-market and demoralizing much of the staff, his vandalism would not be profitable at all, and Random's profits would fall to unprecedented lows. By the time Vitale, too, was replaced, Random's profits would be one one-hundredth of what he had promised—0.1 percent, rather than the 10 percent that he had assured Newhouse his reign would guarantee, at a minimum.

But the pressure for profit had begun to take its toll even before Vitale's arrival. Even though Pantheon wasn't expected to bring in vast amounts, I had to make sure that it would have a reasonable share of bestsellers and other books that would cover the losses often incurred by our intellectual output. With luck, I managed to publish a number of fiction writers I admired, ranging from Marguerite Duras to Anita Brookner, whose books did reach the middle of the bestsellers list. We were also fortunate in making bestsellers of George Kennan's later and very important writings. Essential too was the continued help of Studs Terkel, whose books sold impressively year after year, both as hardcover and paperback bestsellers—his *Working* reached over one million copies in its various editions.

In the sixties and early seventies, our political books had also reached a huge audience, with titles by authors such as Richard Cloward and Frances Fox Piven selling well over half a million copies, and Noam Chomsky, too, reaching a mass audience. I was delighted by the scope of their success, but I knew that it was a sign of the times, of the increased political commitment of universities and political organizations. Books, I felt, were often used as surrogate ballots, especially for ideas that were ahead of the major political parties' platforms. As the political climate in the late seventies and eighties changed, so did the sales of these authors; book sales are an excellent though unstudied indicator of public opinion. While I was determined that the political changes in the U.S. would not affect what we knew we had to publish, I had to spend an increasing amount of time making sure that our financial books were balanced.

* * *

Though difficult, this balancing act could work as long as Bernstein was in charge, who largely shared our left-of-center

RECEIVING MY MA FROM CAMBRIDGE, EARLY 1960S, WITH RICHARD GOODER, MY CAMBRIDGE
ROOMMATE, WHO STAYED ON TO TEACH AT CAMBRIDGE FOR THE REST OF HIS LIFE

WITH MARIA ELENA, SHORTLY AFTER OUR MARRIAGE, IN 1962 (PHOTO: JENNIFER FAY)

WITH GEORGE KENNAN AT THE FRANKFURT BOOK FAIR, AS WE PUBLISHED HIS
THE NUCLEAR DELUSION

DEMONSTRATING AGAINST THE CLOSING OF PANTHEON. LEFT TO RIGHT: KURT VONNEGUT, THE HISTORIAN ARNO MAYER, AND STUDS TERKEL, JANUARY 1990 (PHOTO: AP IMAGES/LEDERHANDLER)

WORKING AT HOME WITH STUDS ON THE MANUSCRIPT OF *RACE*, HIS FIRST BOOK AT THE NEW PRESS.
LEFT IS DAWN DAVIS, MY THEN ASSISTANT, NOW AN EDITOR AT HARPERCOLLINS

THE NEW PRESS STAFF, SHORTLY AFTER WE STARTED, IN 1994. *PUBLISHERS WEEKLY* USED THE PHOTO TO SHOW THAT RACIAL DIVERSITY IN PUBLISHING WAS POSSIBLE. DIANE WACHTELL, TO MY RIGHT, IS NOW EXECUTIVE DIRECTOR OF THE NEW PRESS. (PHOTO: PUBLISHERS WEEKLY)

A RECENT FAMILY PHOTO: MY DAUGHTERS ANYA, ON THE LEFT, AND NATALIA, WITH THEIR HUSBANDS PHILIPPE SANDS AND JOSEPH STIGLITZ AND NATALIA'S CHILDREN, KATYA, LEO, AND LARA

A RECENT PHOTO TAKEN IN MILAN WHEN I WAS AWARDED THE GRISANE CAVOUR BOLLATI PRIZE, GIVEN TO A PUBLISHER EACH YEAR FOR HIS LIFE'S WORK. THE FIRST AWARD WAS GIVEN TO THE GERMAN HANS MAGNUS ENZENSBERGER; MINE WAS SECOND; AND THE THIRD WENT TO ANTIOINE GALLIMARD, GASTON GALLIMARD'S GRANDSON.

views. Bob was very involved in starting Human Rights Watch; originally a far smaller organization than the huge and effective operation it has now become, the group would meet monthly in the Random conference room. But as we were to find out in time, Si Newhouse appreciated neither Bob's commitment to authors such as Russia's dissident Andrei Sakharov, nor mine to America's critics. Instead, the far more conservative Newhouse brought to Random authors such as Joe McCarthy's right-hand man, Roy Cohn, and later Donald Trump, the icon of speculative capitalism.

All this would come to a head very rapidly at the end of 1989. Once Bernstein was replaced by Vitale, it was only a question of time before Pantheon would be eliminated. Logically, to my Cartesian mind, there was no reason why this should happen. Our list was becoming stronger and stronger, with sales approaching $20 million per year—admittedly only a tiny percentage of Random's overall sales, but infinitely more than the $1 million per year that Pantheon had reached when Random bought it.

Our last catalogue was probably the best I had ever put together. Ironically, we had just signed on the first of the Bart Simpson books. I had published Matt Groening's very funny *Life in Hell* books of cartoons, and he had proposed this latest venture to us. We had seen the initial installments of the TV series weeks before leaving, and I felt sure we had a huge success on our hands. Our sales were increasing as quickly as any stockholder could have asked for and were helping to build a backlist that would sell for years to come.

But the success of these titles were no longer important. What mattered were two completely different but crucial issues: Vitale wanted each of our titles to be profitable, while I insisted on the classic publishing assumption that the successful books should subsidize those that made less money. Later, Vitale would explain in a newspaper interview that this philosophy had to be eradicated; if Pantheon could get away with doing this, the others would insist on similar rights. His solution was to have me eliminate two-thirds of our front list—assuming that the remaining third would be the most profitable. The idea behind this was also to fire two-thirds of the staff as well. But Newhouse had another agenda, helpfully suggested by Vitale: Why publish all those books on the Left and not more on the Right? Vitale would later deny having ever said this, but this was clearly a major demand.[28]

I did not realize that I was facing an implacable ideology. In spite of all the rumors that had swirled around us after Bernstein's firing, I couldn't conceive that Pantheon's end was near. Nor did I understand the degree of fiscal trickery that was going on: Not having access to the corporate books, I didn't know that we were being charged for the expenses of other divisions that had nothing to do with us, or that we were being billed for expenses we never incurred—I found I was being charged for a car, even though I have never learned how to drive. Most important, much of our backlist was declared to have no value and was written off by the accountants as having no future sales potential. This would effect most of the books that we depended on to make us profitable.

---

[28] The other large conglomerates have since also begun right-wing imprints. Now, publishers as varied as Rupert Murdoch's HarperCollins and Penguin have the pleasure of publishing books that that promote their political beliefs and which, in the Reagan-Bush years, would indeed be profitable as well.

These tricks applied only to us and not to other parts of Random, and were used by Vitale to show that Pantheon and Pantheon alone was losing millions. He used the numbers to convince both the Random staff, and later the press, that Pantheon was too expensive to keep on. It was the actuarial equivalent of a mugging.

While I was busy battling with the accountants and showing them the impossibility of Vitale's demands, my younger colleagues, schooled in the politics of 1968, spent their evenings otherwise. They wrote to all of our authors and to many others explaining what was happening: It led to a growing protest, full-page ads in our support, and finally a gathering of several hundred people in front of the Random House building on East Fiftieth Street. Demonstrators included Studs Terkel, who flew in from Chicago, and many of our other authors, but also those from other publishers, such as Kurt Vonnegut, who understood the issues that were at stake. All these people, by the way, were covertly photographed by the Random House public-relations department.

Publishers Weekly, the trade journal, ran sympathetic articles and editorials—until it was threatened by Vitale with the loss of all future ads from Random House, as I later learned from authoritative sources. Since all of Pantheon's editors had decided to resign en masse and I had joined them in their decision, the effect was dramatic. People usually decide to stay on, at least for a while, and see if they can find an accommodation with a new management. Such a collective departure had never happened before in publishing, and it effectively dramatized what Vitale's actions meant.

Publishers in Europe also rallied to our defense, sending letters and petitions. After my departure, Spanish publishers banded together to invite me to Barcelona, where they gave a gala dinner in my honor and showed how much Pantheon's emphasis on European writers and issues had meant to them— a moving contrast to the way my own Random House colleagues had behaved.

The demand that I fire two-thirds of the staff had been the effective end of Pantheon. I had assumed that our colleagues at Random and Knopf, seeing that the integrity of their publishing was equally threatened, would rally to our defense. But during the weeks in which these events unfolded, not a single editor from Random and Knopf had come to me privately to ask what was really going on. I assume that they were strongly discouraged from doing so. All but two courageous Knopf editors signed a kind of loyalty oath, written by two of the most vociferously anti-Pantheon editors, but clearly with Vitale's backing, proclaiming that quality and profitability were inextricably intertwined. Within a few years, a number of those who signed would discover that they, too, were threatened and would leave as well.

* * *

I expected the press to cover the whole controversy fairly and once again exhibited the innocence underlying so many of my reformist expectations: The media might well be unfair in their coverage of many political issues, but on the question of cultural diversity and press freedom, surely they would be fair if not favorable to our arguments? After all, our books were well known and had often been well received by the leading papers. But I was told by insiders that the *New York Times* reporter assigned to cover our story was instructed to write in a hostile fashion—"Schiffrin has an undeserved halo," he was told. Accordingly, the *Times* and others bought the Random line that publishing was too important a business to be left in the hands of intellectuals. Bob Bernstein was tarred with the same brush, in spite of having been a spectacularly successful businessman. Following the line set by the Random public-relations department, we were told by the press that you need tough businessmen like Alberto Vitale to run what was now being called the publishing "industry." Not only did most of the coverage follow this line, but stories were placed accordingly: When James Michener, Random House's most successful author, spoke of possibly leaving the house over this issue, the story was placed on the *Times*' shipping page, next to the listings of cargo ships leaving the New York harbor. When Michener was persuaded to stay, it was covered on the book page.

At one point, I joked with my colleagues that we were being treated like Nicaraguans. We had become public enemies, proof that any opposition to full-blown corporate control was subversive. Indeed, many of the stories seemed aimed at making sure that no one would ever hire me—when the director of the Harvard University Press asked if I'd consider succeeding him, a full-fledged campaign was carried out by Random House to make sure I wasn't offered the job. People on the search committee told me of calls from Random editors with links to Harvard who suggested that offering me the job would doom the Press, would lead to the kind of financial losses that Vitale's publicity people had invented. In the year following the end of Pantheon, I would get only one very tentative job offer—from an old colleague whose firm, Basic Books, would soon undergo the same kind of transformation that had been intended for us.

Meanwhile, not too long after I left Pantheon, I got two letters from Si Newhouse congratulating me on the fact that two of the books on my final list at Pantheon—Dale Maharidge's *And Their Children After Them* (a sequel to James Agee's *Let Us Now Praise Famous Men*) and Art Spiegelman's *Maus*, which would end up selling in the millions—had won Pulitzer prizes.

We were no longer in the McCarthy period but our struggle against the new ideology of maximizing profit, and against the insistence that each book had to make an *immediate* profit, was seen as a new form of subversion, and we were attacked with many of the same kinds of smears and pressures. Our former colleagues were not literally threatened, as they would have been in the fifties, but it was made clear to them that they were expected to toe the company line. (One of the two editors who had refused to sign the loyalty oath was, in fact, the daughter of one of the Hollywood figures who had suffered during the McCarthy period.) Capitalism was to be defended not from the Communists but from the internal enemies who argued that the maximization of profit was not the proper goal. It would be made clear to the industry as well as to the public at large that these "intellectuals" were purveyors of a dangerous doctrine, which suggested that values other than profit might not only exist but be as important. We were not threatened with Congressional hearings, but the private sector and the press were successful in suggesting that we were not only incompetent but dangerous to hire. The new ideology had to be defended as forcefully as the old Cold War consensus had been.

A couple of years later, the scenario would play out again when Newhouse decided to fire Bob Gottlieb, who had been head of Knopf during much of my time at Random House, for not living up to profit expectations after being named the editor of Conde Nast's *New Yorker*. The Newhouse propaganda machine came up with a rationale similar to their attack on us: that Gottlieb had been too faithful to the brilliant editorship of his predecessor William Shawn, and once again the press echoed this line. The profitable decades during which the *New Yorker* had published John Hersey's *Hiroshima*, Rachel Carson's environmental classic *Silent Spring*, and Jonathan Schell's writings on Vietnam were aberrations, it was explained. The true nature of the magazine was to be found in the slight and gossipy tone of its earliest years. The new editor, Tina Brown, since replaced as well, could be trusted to reestablish the old values and presumably increase advertising revenue. Newhouse would also be freed, during her tenure, of the magazine's crusading journalism.

I sometimes wonder whether my old Social Democrat-reformist origins had led me to trust private enterprise too much. But I feel persuaded that it is also capitalism itself that has changed, rather than just myself. All of us, from Bennett Cerf on, shared the same optimism about corporate takeover. We all believed that the ownership would change but that the people running the firm would stay the same. Had not the classic studies, such as those of Berle and Means, showed that it was management that ran corporations; that made all the crucial decisions? But in assuming as he did that RCA would still allow him to choose the books he liked, Cerf—like the rest of us—had failed to appreciate the degree to which capitalism had been transformed. People bought firms not because they gave a damn about what they produced, but because buying them could make more money—often, by selling off parts of what they'd bought, or by firing vast numbers of employees who were "no longer needed." Publishers bought each other up not because they actually needed new imprints, but because this was a way of showing the required annual growth figures. If you bought a firms, you could integrate its backlist into yours and fire much if not all of its staff. Newhouse's handling of Random had been but a small-time example of what was going on a much vaster scale in the economy as a whole, throughout the world.

* * *

Not only publishing but the other liberal professions, as they were once called, were being affected. My Yale classmates who were now lawyers and doctors would complain to me about a similar transformation of their roles. Lawyers were expected to become "rainmakers" and bring in high-paying clients, and law firms would become incredibly profitable. Doctors would find themselves making medical decisions imposed on them either by insurance companies or by hospital administrations, whose primary concern was money, not health. Their salaries skyrocketed, but their freedom disappeared.

When I started in publishing, salaries in many firms resembled those in universities: a senior editor made a professor's salary, a beginner the same as his campus equivalent. The highest salary in British publishing when I first visited England was a notorious £10,000. By the mid-1990s, million-dollar salaries had become common in the corporatized firms, and the salaries of many editors were tied closely to financial results. Conversely, profit-and-loss statements were kept for each editor to gauge how much money their books made. From the start of their careers, editors were made aware that their future depended not on the quality of the books they took on, but on the books' profitability. Final decisions about which books to acquire were increasingly taken on by the sales and financial people, so that even if an editor tried to play his traditional role, he would be reined in. An iron mask of profitability was fixed on the face of a profession that once had been able to take risks and discover new talent. For the first time in history, ideas were judged not by their importance but by their profit potential.

Very quickly, the nature of American and British publishing—which now largely shared ownership—was altered beyond recognition. Lists such as that of HarperCollins, once rich in all the classic fields of knowledge, from theology to art history, soon were shedding these less-lucrative areas. Instead, publishing redefined itself as part of the "entertainment industry" and sought TV and movie tie-ins galore. Occasionally a book of serious history or sociology would still appear, but in most cases these turned out to be from contracts written years before that somehow had not been cancelled.

As I left Pantheon, I realized that the chances of ever being able to do again what we had accomplished there over the last thirty years were very slight. There seemed no reasonable possibility of finding a major firm that would allow me to do what we had done, and the few remaining intellectual branches of the large conglomerates, such as Basic Books at HarperCollins and the Free Press at Simon & Schuster, the latter something of a right-wing counterpart to Pantheon, were soon transformed into more commercial ventures, just as Vitale had intended to do with Pantheon. To be sure, university presses might still try to fill this vacuum, but they, too, were under increasing pressure—more and more of them were also now expected to make profits.

There seemed no obvious solution within the existing system. For years I had wondered whether there might not be the equivalent of a university press without a university's backing, and without the relatively conservative effect of faculty decisionmaking on every book. I knew that many of the most intellectually exciting books that we had published over the years had been turned down by universities, which all too often had become bastions of the status quo. I looked again at a statement I'd written for the Harvard job, detailing my ideas on the future direction of the press, and I began to think it could be an outline for an independent, not-for-profit publishing house, one that would be free of profit pressures from stockholders.

In my last weeks at Pantheon, I had begun to work out a prospectus that we would use to seek support from foundations. After all, they had seen that commercial radio and television needed not-for-profit alternatives such as the Public Broadcasting System (PBS) and National Public Radio (NPR). Nearly all of classical music, and much of the theatre, were likewise performed by not-for-profits. A similar case could be made for independent publishing. The controversy over Pantheon had guaranteed that everyone was at least aware of the basic issues and the need for at least one left-of-center, mainstream publisher would have some appeal to liberal funders. I began the process of presenting my ideas to the leading foundations.

Most important, our authors had shown incredible loyalty. Only two elected to remain with Random, and people such as Studs Terkel pledged to our new enterprise, even when offered vast amounts by others. I didn't have the money to keep most of my former colleagues, however, and urged them to take the authors with whom they had worked.[29] But there were enough to form the core of a new house—The New Press, as we unimaginatively called it.

My old optimism and trust in America made me sure we could somehow succeed. The idea seemed so reasonable that I was sure others would see the sense in it, just as, when I was a teenager, I'd felt sure that others would understand that Socialism made the best sense. Years later, even my closest friends admitted that they had not thought we would pull it off. But in spite of the difficulties of having to set up a nonexisting organization from my living room, and of waiting endlessly for foundations to decide whether to support us or not, Diane Wachtell, my former assistant, and I finally succeeded in setting up shop, roughly a year after I'd left Pantheon.

I have told the story of the ensuing years elsewhere. Suffice it to say that seventeen years later, as of this writing, The New Press continues to publish—now, some eighty books a year—and plays

---

[29] One who did so was Wendy Wulf, the editor of the Simpsons cartoon books by Matt Groening that we had been working on when I left Pantheon. Those books would go on to sell millions, which would have made Pantheon for a while the most profitable part of Random House—if Groening hadn't moved with Wendy to another house. Another of our senior editors, Sara Bershtel, would in time establish at Metropolitan Books a list very close to what we had done at Pantheon. Among the authors with whom she had worked at Pantheon, Barbara Ehrenreich became an enormous success, selling over a million copies of her bestseller *Nickel and Dimed.*

much the same role that Pantheon used to. Of course, we lack the infinite resources that we had at Random House. But part of the irony of the Pantheon experience has been that we rarely needed Newhouse's billions. For the most part, the books we wanted to publish did not command huge advances.

This remained the case with us, as it did with an increasing number of new, small independent firms. One of my pleasures in starting afresh was to see the growing ranks of small publishers taking on the fields that had been abandoned by the larger houses: They were now the prime purveyors of poetry, translation, and new literary fiction. Most were run by young people who had seen what commercial publishing had become and had decided they could do better. There were some major hurdles: Their access to bookstores was severely limited, and none of us had the resources to commission expensive, long-range projects. The small publishers nonetheless have become an important alternative in the U.S. and overseas.

* * *

A few years ago, I contrasted this development with European publishing, which had kept to its traditional profile. In France at that time, although two-thirds of publishing was controlled by two vast conglomerates, there were still enough major independent houses to set a higher tone for the field and to force the conglomerates to continue the kind of serious publishing that had largely disappeared from the U.S. and England. Then, in 2003, I decided to spend a year working in France, and I was shocked to see the American model not only emulated but exceeded. One of the two ruling conglomerates, Vivendi, had tried too hard to follow the lead of the Americans, and had bought up so many media firms at such excessive prices that it very quickly faced bankruptcy. Rather than insist that Vivendi's component parts be sold off to different buyers, the French government urged the country's other leading conglomerate, Hachette, to buy up its rival. The resulting behemoth would have controlled two-thirds of French publishing. In certain key fields, such as textbooks, reference books, and distribution, it would have amounted to a near-total monopoly.

Reading about it in the French papers, I was astonished to see that this merger was proceeding unopposed. No one involved—not publishers, nor the press, nor authors—was complaining about a merger that would have put most of French intellectual life into the hands of what was basically an arms manufacturer. Finally, French booksellers, aware of what such a monopoly might do to their sales terms, complained to the European Union antitrust commission in Brussels. After a year of careful study, the commission prevented a complete takeover of Vivendi, but it did allow Hachette to buy a hefty 42 percent of its former rival.

In the meanwhile, the number of major independent firms had sharply diminished. One of France's most distinguished publishers, Le Seuil, had been bought up by another conglomerate, led by a publisher of picture books, La Martinière, which had raised money for the deal from such varied sources as Chanel, Werthheimer, and the *Chicago Tribune*. Le Seuil's program underwent a classic capitalist transformation: Every book must henceforth be profitable, its editors were told. When, in a radio debate with the new owner, I asked if he really meant to follow such a disastrous policy, I was assured that this indeed was the name of the game. France showed how quickly, with all of its traditional insistence on "*L'exception Française,*" it could follow the globalized example.

As a result of this kind of conglomerate control, the French, too, soon saw the growth of small independent publishers who began to take on authors like Chomsky and even Hobsbawm. Just as I had found partners among the young editors in the large European firms when I had started out at Pantheon, I now found, in these tiny new firms, a new generation of like-minded partners for The New Press.

But while this new wave was encouraging, it was, unfortunately, due to the fact that globalization had taken over world publishing along with everything else. The ramparts of European culture were being overwhelmed by the new forces of international capitalism, with the all-too-willing collaboration not only of the publishers themselves but of the media. As if this wasn't bad enough, a similar takeover of the press in 2003 put two-thirds of all French newspapers and magazines in the control of arms manufacturers, firms whose main customer was the French government itself. Once again, the all-powerful media conglomerate Hachette was in the middle of it all, along with Dassault, the warplane manufacturer, whose owner publicly explained that he had bought the venerable daily *Le Figaro* so as to have a paper that would express his own opinions.

In the United States, conglomerate ownership of the media showed itself to be even more dangerous. While the press had been largely owned by Republicans, it had nonetheless prided itself on a certain independence and a willingness to criticize the government—even, as in the famous Watergate case, to bring it down. But after 9/11, a frightening new era of self-censorship began. Much of this was due to the shock of the attack and the understandable surge of patriotism that followed. But the Bush government wanted much more than that and knew how to get it. Even before the attacks on Afghanistan, Condoleezza Rice, who was then Bush's national security advisor, called into her office the heads of all the television networks and told them that the government did not want to see pictures of wounded civilians on their screens. Aware of how television had helped to end the Vietnam War, and presumably aware of the Iraq invasion to come, Bush wanted to be sure that the press would be compliant. Journalists were "embedded" with the troops they were to cover. Then, in 2003, the Bush administration assured itself of further control of the media by having the FCC deregulate cross-media ownership to an unprecedented degree, a move worth billions to the ever-enlarging media conglomerates. Among the FCC's petitioners requesting the loosened regulations were Rupert Murdoch and the *New York Times*—which did not give more than the most token coverage to the FCC hearings that were meant to grant them historic concessions. And, coincidentally, practically none of the major news outlets raised any of the obvious and crucial questions concerning the government's lies about weapons of mass destruction for the crucial first two years of the war. At one notorious press conference, Bush insisted eight times that there were known links between Saddam Hussein and al-Qaeda without a single one of the journalists present daring to question him. As a result, close to 80 percent of those who voted for Bush in his second election were persuaded that there had indeed been WMDs in Iraq.

Though it is true that in the past the press has usually followed the government's line on foreign policy, book publishers
have, at least in recent years, shown more independence. During
the Vietnam War, just about every publisher, including the largest
houses, brought out numerous books critical of the government.
But during those important first two years of the war in Iraq, not
a single large house published a book critical of Bush's war. I was
so astonished by this that I asked the editor of *Publishers Weekly*
whether I had missed some titles, but I was assured that none had
appeared.

These could hardly have been commercial decisions. After
all, more than half of the country had voted against Bush, and the
antiwar movement had a large and determined membership. But
the only books to appear came from the small, independent publishers. Shortly after the attacks of September 11, 2001, Seven
Stories Press, a small independent in New York, published a book
by Noam Chomsky called *9/11*, which immediately sold 100,000
copies, showing the potential audience for critical books. But the
large publishers belonged to conglomerates that, for the most
part, had other media holdings that depended on the administration's largesse. This clear form of self-censorship persisted until
even the leading papers felt obliged to publish mea culpas, while
continuing to be extremely cautious in their coverage of the wars.

To compare even a conservative French newspaper's coverage of Afghanistan or Iraq to an American newspaper's coverage,
meanwhile, is to visit not two different continents, but two different worlds. The French coverage, of course, echoes its government's foreign policy, one that shows how far the Europeans still
are from Bush's America. When French and American positions
coincide, as they did recently in Haiti during the overthrow of

Jean-Bertrand Aristide, then so does the coverage. The articles on Haiti in *Le Figaro* could easily have been mistaken for those in the *New York Times.*

To be truly independent, a newspaper is helped greatly by being free of conglomerate control, as we have seen in the last few years. This has been made abundantly clear in England, where the newspapers belonging to Murdoch have consistently attacked the opponents of the Iraq war and toed their party line with fervor—and with a total disregard for what was actually happening. By contrast, the *Guardian* has been savagely critical of Tony Blair, not just on Iraq but on domestic issues as well. The contrast is partly due to the fact that the *Guardian,* and its Sunday edition the *Observer,* both belong to the Scott Trust, a foundation that has allowed them total editorial independence. This is not to say these papers have been completely free of commercial pressures. Like all of the English press, with the noted exception of the *Financial Times,* they have gone considerably down-market, but the editorial integrity has been preserved. They have played an important role in rallying the growing opposition to Blair.

But American readers have had no such newspapers to rely upon. Instead, in the U.S., the Web has played a vital role in disseminating information missing in the mainstream media, with much of its foreign news coming from the *Guardian* and other foreign papers. Important as the Web has been, its independent sites are unable to send out reporters to see what is really happening. They have to depend on the foreign papers that have had the resources to do so.

As we have seen, publishing itself has been badly limited by its conglomerate ownership. It took two long years for the major firms to begin to publish the books, many of which became bestsellers, that outlined the lies of the Bush administration. I am convinced that if the media and the publishers had done this from Day One, Bush would not have been able to push the country into the disastrous war in Iraq. While newspapers and broadcast media play a more important role, book publishing is also crucial. It can give authors the time and space to develop a complex argument, and to give the other media new, in-depth information. Books are the ideal way to reach the broadest public with different and dissenting views that would not have originated within the mainstream media itself.

Once again, we see the importance of existing outside the network of conglomerate control. The realm outside such control used to be inhabited by small, family-owned publishers, but these have largely disappeared. The main hope today comes from the new wave of small independent publishers, largely not-for-profits, whether de jure or de facto. Firms like Seven Stories, Haymarket, and the publisher of this book are playing an increasingly important role in making debate possible, though of course they lack the resources of the larger firms.

* * *

Concurrent with the rise of the small independents, however, here and in Europe, there has been a sharp decrease in the number of publishers that are part of what is now called "civil society." Churches, unions, and political parties all used to have important publishing programs. These played a crucial role during the Vietnam War. In the U.S., Beacon Press, owned by the Unitarian Church, is one of the few such to survive. In Europe, ironically, even the unions and co-ops have decided that their publishing was insufficiently profitable and that funds would be better invested elsewhere. This shortsighted view has led to the disappearance of the important newspapers linked to the labour movement as well. The names of the papers are still there, but their politics have changed, often rightward. The result has cost the unions and their members far more than the money they had invested in media of their own.

One can only hope that the experience of the last few years will show people the importance of independent media. Even groups on the far right, such as the National Rifle Association, were active in opposing George Bush's planned giveaways to the major media conglomerates—the 3 million letters and e-mails of protest sent to the Congress to protest the FCC deregulation of cross-media ownership did not come from the Left alone, but from a broad range of people who realized the importance of maintaining some kind of diversity and local control in the media.

There has been one hopeful sign in recent months: The Knight Ridder newspaper chain was recently sold off because it was making a mere 19 percent annual profit. Clearly, no profit is large enough to satisfy owners in today's capitalism, just as there is no limit to the salaries that management feel justified in paying themselves. The sale of the Knight Ridder chain inevitably involved closing down many of the least profitable papers, though presumably even these were still making enough money to stay afloat. However, with foundation help, a move was initiated by the journalists working for the endangered papers to try to buy the papers themselves and keep them going, as not-for-profits if need be. Such an approach would be a healthy return to the days when newspapers were started with their own staffs in control. Papers do not need to cost a fortune, or to make one. When I recently visited the city of Oslo, which has a population of well under one million people, it had fourteen dailies, ranging from anarchist to conservative. The press does not have to be an expensive, capital intensive operation, any more than book publishing does. News and opinions can be disseminated without conglomerate investment or control, as is the case with radio as well.

Our experience with The New Press showed that with relatively little money (the grants we received our first year totaled less than one million dollars), one can re-create the kind of independent publishing that used to exist in the U.S. and in England. It will be interesting to see if similar experiments can succeed in the press and in other media. But the very fact that new forms of ownership for the Knight Ridder papers had been discussed is in itself encouraging. It shows that the old Socialist ideas of workers' control and non-capitalist ownership are not only interesting as theories, but can be viable solutions to the many problems created by today's economic system.

Felix Rohatyn, the noted liberal financier and former U.S. ambassador to France, recently wrote in the *International Herald Tribune* that corporations should think beyond the value of their stocks and the profits they make. Using the newly fashionable idea of stakeholders—all those who have an interest in a firm—he argues that companies should consider "the employees, communities, customers and suppliers" in their decision-making. At a time when global corporate giants like Wal-Mart run roughshod over the rights of most of the people Rohatyn identifies, his point is worth taking. But fond as I am of reformist ideas, I must ask what would happen to the shares of such companies. Surely Wall Street would urge investors to stay away from anyone who didn't put maximization of profit at the top of their agenda.

Businesses have been so successful at undermining any countervailing power that government regulation has increasingly proved ineffective. It is in this extreme climate that the old arguments for public ownership make increasing sense. If Western countries wish to hold on to any of their manufacturing, public ownership is an obvious answer. When, after the Second World War, many major firms such as Renault and Volkswagen were nationalized, the Right argued that precisely because they were so successful, they could easily be reconverted to private ownership. But the problem now is not simply being profitable, it is continuing to supply jobs and income to a country's own citizens. Any European car firm can become more profitable by moving its plants to Slovakia, where workers are paid a quarter of the wages prevailing in Western Europe. Thus, Slovakia now makes more cars per capita than any European country. But this also helps to assure that other countries will continue to have high unemployment rates and all the costs that go with that, both human and financial. In the long run, countries would do far better with publicly owned, not-for-profit firms than with the current situation, where not only manufacturing jobs but service jobs as well are moving overseas at an incredible rate.

These are purely practical arguments; they do not address the underlying issues of equality and fairness that were always at the base of the Socialist case and that used to be accepted by much of the Left as well. What is unfortunate is that these arguments are never voiced in the United States. There is no debate based on the Socialist case, relevant as it may be. Politics has moved so far to the right since the seventies that the Republicans can—and do—accuse the Democrats of being Socialists or even Communists when the Democrats propose the slightest improvement in the welfare state or in the increasingly inequitable tax program. Funded by the same large corporations, the Democrats have failed to offer any meaningful opposition in recent years. Having a Socialist argument to their left, even if its chances of winning are most unlikely, would at least help to bring the overall debate back to a more realistic confrontation of real alternatives.

Clearly, in recent decades our attempts to publish authors that might open up the public discussion have hardly been successful. But as the capitalist reality becomes ever more extreme and threatening, as much to the middle class as to the increasing numbers of the poor, there may yet be a willingness to listen more openly and to consider arguments—such as Rohatyn's—that a few years ago would have gone unheeded.

Happily, the situation is very different outside the United States. Increasingly, countries have begun to resist an American foreign policy that has sought to privatize most of the world's resources. Using the World Bank, America has insisted that countries give up their control of primary resources, even of water, in exchange for badly needed international aid. The results of these policies have been so disastrous that more and more nations have rebelled, especially in Latin America. In much of the world the old Socialist assumption that natural resources belong to the population as a whole have always been accepted. Country after country has realized that the foreign firms exploiting their oil, etc., were paying them a pittance of the products' value. Ironically,

Bolivia's current share of its oil profits, 18 percent (according to President Evo Morales), is identical to what British Petroleum was paying the Iranians in the 1950s, one of the practices that in time led to the overthrow of the client governments we had installed to protect our interests. While Morales and Venezuela's Hugo Chávez are understandably worrying Washington, no one here has been willing to ask the obvious question: Why shouldn't these countries control their own wealth? Mexico, Venezuela, Norway, and, for a while, even the Canadian province of Saskatchewan had all nationalized their oil. The question should not be "Why have these countries done this?" but "Why have we never considered such an alternative in the U.S.?"

Clearly, it is utopian to think that America might ever join the rest of the world in asking those questions. Or why the peace dividend that so many of us had expected after the end of the Cold War never materialized. The overwhelming defense budget makes it very hard to limit those whom, like the present administration, assume that military force will solve all of our problems—an argument still being made even in the face of the Iraqi debacle. One is forced to ask whether America can ever escape the pattern with which it responds to change overseas.

The current massive and unwarranted arrests of thousands of innocent Muslim Americans is in keeping with America's history over the last century. When the Russian revolution took place, America's immediate response was to crack down on domestic radicals, since there was very little it could do to stop the Bolshevik revolution. The infamous Palmer Raids that followed the First World War saw thousands of supposed Bolshevik sympathizers, as well as assorted left-wingers, summarily arrested and deported. In a manner closely resembling those adopted decades later by Bush's first attorney general, John Ashcroft, due process was forgotten and civil liberties trampled.

The McCarthy period elicited a similar reaction to change overseas that we found we couldn't control. Though America had won the war, the Communists were taking over more and more countries. McCarthy's accusation that the Democrats had "lost" China was based on the same assumptions that nowadays makes the Right feel that they can reconquer the "lost" Middle East: that these countries were meant to be under our control, not open to the influence or seizure by Communists or Islamists. In these instances, America was supposed to be all-powerful and if things weren't working out, it had to be due to traitors and subversives at home. Joe McCarthy's charge of "Twenty Years of Treason," aimed at Roosevelt and Truman, was a frank statement of these assumptions—the Democrats' weakness, not the forces of change following the war and China's revolution, was responsible for the Communist victories,. These are ideas that still exist in the Bush administration.

It is too much to assume that rational discourse and good historical analysis would have abolished such powerful forces. But it wouldn't have hurt to have a bit more of this kind of questioning, some form of national debate contesting these assumptions. In recent years it has been troubling both that so little has been published along these lines, and that so little attention has been paid to what *has* appeared. The dozens of books that we have published on these issues have received very few reviews; the self-censorship that kept the press from questioning the Iraq war has largely extended to the realm of ideas as well.

America has emerged from the past eras of repression, the twenties and fifties, and presumably will gradually get over the Bush years, as the recent Supreme Court decisions on Guantánamo and the 2006 congressional elections suggest. Or, at least, my old reformist optimism still makes me believe this. But what is worrying is the damage done to the structural ramparts of our democracy. In each of those previous historical periods, both the courts and the media were targeted. Clearly Bush is well aware of the importance of these limits on his power and ideas. He has done all within his power, and a lot beyond the Constitutional constraints on the presidency to curb those who oppose him. The strength of the independent media has also been severely limited and much of what has been destroyed may never be rebuilt. This is among the major issues we will need to face in the coming years.

History has always been my major interest, both as a student and as an editor. So I suppose it's only natural that I should look at my experience in the context of past years. To be sure, I was an overly optimistic teenager, but the immediate postwar period was one in which many—if not most—people in America also thought that things would be much better. In part it was the feeling that, after all the destruction wrought by the war, we needed to rebuild a better world. Reconstruction was a key term, a kind of debt the living owed to all those dead. But we also realized that the war had brought America to its full potential. Its productivity had skyrocketed. The problem of "underutilized capacity"—the Left's perennial critique of capitalism—was gone. Everyone was employed, even women and blacks. The economy was carefully planned, and even though it was not Socialist planning, it showed how much more could be accomplished by the government when the large firms no longer decided how the economy would function.

The memories of the Depression years were still very much with us. I remember that the cartoons in the *Saturday Evening Post*, which I read religiously in the late 1940s, after graduating from comics, still featured the bum begging at the back door. The image of those thousands of jobless who criss-crossed mid-America was still very much a part of our collective memory. That it was the war that had brought full employment was understood by all, as was the determination not to return to the dark thirties.

I realized, well before I had read Werner Sombart's classic 1906 book *Why Is There No Socialism in the United States?*, that my dreams would not be fulfilled. But I was enough of a reformer to settle for Truman's Fair Deal as an interim measure. I was not the only one to hope for a continuation of the New Deal. Everything seemed to point to its revival. In my logic-ridden brain, I could foresee no reason why progress should not continue.

None of us, Socialists or capitalists, foresaw what would happen after the end of colonialism's draconian rule. The best the Socialist International could propose to us in the fifties was that we celebrate something with the incredibly mealymouthed name of Dependent Peoples Freedom Day. But that did not include making plans for the postcolonial world, giving needed help to those countries to develop healthy economies, or helping them to avoid falling under the equally exploitative control of private firms, as happened in the Belgian Congo. Corruption, private armies, and ethnic conflicts would all follow, encouraging an endless flow of illegal immigrants to Europe, just as Mexican poverty encouraged a similar emigration to the United States.

It's not as if some policies to limit the damage were not possible. The Swedish Socialists ruled early on that all immigrants would have to join trade unions, assuring that there would be no "black economy," no competition between underpaid foreigners and local workers. So it may not be a coincidence that Sweden is the only Nordic country that has not spawned a right-wing, nationalist, anti-immigrant party. In country after country, economic competition has helped to create or revive racist feelings, which have been exploited by the Right in Europe as well as here in the United States. The phenomenon of Reagan Democrats has not been limited to the U.S. Workers everywhere have become more conservative as they have become more prosperous. In America, it is now the Republicans who accuse the Democrats of encouraging class warfare when Democrats talk about the growing inequity of incomes.

Workers' salaries in the U.S. are now 10 percent below those obtained in the early seventies. At the same time, the top 1 percent earn a fifth of the total national income and own close to one-third of all the wealth. The top 5 percent have close to half of all the nation's wealth and are, of course, the prime beneficiaries of the Bush tax cuts.[30]

In Europe, public opinion has still maintained some of its Socialist values, arguing for more equity and a decent minimum wage. Apart from the England of Thatcher and Blair, the differences between rich and poor are nowhere near as great as in the United States, although the new capitalist governments in Eastern Europe and Russia are doing their best to catch up with us.

These economic changes toward greater inequality have been reinforced since the Reagan years. But they were also helped along earlier by the evolution of the Cold War and its impact on domestic policy. In the fifties, all of us, liberals and the few remaining Socialists, underestimated the effect that the Cold War would have, not only on our reformist expectations but on the country's own democratic climate.

---

[30] Figures are from the *New York Times*, October 15, 2006.

Looking back, we can see that each time domestic policy looked as if it might turn leftward, it was halted by wars overseas. Korea put an end to Truman's Fair Deal hopes just as Vietnam ended Johnson's ambitious War on Poverty. The hopes for a "peace dividend" after the collapse of Soviet Communism evaporated without any debate, and when George W. Bush was elected, inheriting a thriving economy, one could see his administration's desperate search for a new enemy until they were saved by 9/11. We've forgotten how determined Bush was in his first years to paint China as the new threat, to create endless provocations against Beijing until Osama bin Laden put all of that on the back burner.

The decades in which I've lived have not been happy ones politically. Europe enjoyed what is now recalled as thirty glorious years after the end of the Second World War, but it too has suffered endless colonial wars. Having had too few colonies of our own, we had to borrow some of Europe's old colonies to defend, from Vietnam to Iraq. We also did our best with our own backyard, from Eisenhower to the present. As we see civilian casualties in Iraq passing the 100,000 mark, we forget that twice that number were killed in the civil wars that we imposed on tiny Guatemala.

So the past sixty years have not been the ideal time to hope for vast social reforms. Yet again, there was no reason to assume that the nature of America's capitalism would change so dramatically—not only that the large firms would get bigger and bigger but that a whole new form of capitalism would develop, in which investment firms would buy companies basically to strip their assets; that the less-profitable segments would be sold off or shut down and the financial pages would crow about the "savings" made by firing thousands of workers; that the words "hostile takeover" would become a part of our vocabulary.

In high school, when I worked late at night in the Eighth Street Bookstore, I did not realize that it, and 90 percent of New York's bookstores, were doomed. The process started when the new discount stores like Korvette's, now long forgotten, began to sell books at far lower prices, sometimes as loss leaders to lure customers through their doors. It was a strategy that was perfected and expanded by the new bookstore chains.

This development was not inevitable. In many European countries, such as France and Germany, governments set a strict limit on discounting, and Paris has many more bookstores than New York did in 1945. There are so many in the neighborhood where I now live that I am unable to look at them all, in spite of a lifetime's habit of compulsive browsing.

The same applies to my own profession, where the endless takeovers of publishing houses were not written in stone—though the inheritance laws helped enormously in killing off the old family-owned firms. One of the few remaining important independent publishers, W. W. Norton, survived as such by letting each new generation of its executives own the companies' shares, a solution that could have been adopted by others. To be sure, in America and elsewhere, there has been widespread growth of small independent firms, but as I have said, these have very limited resources and find it increasingly difficult to compete in a world dominated by the bestseller-centered chain stores.

I am often accused of excessive pessimism when I mention all this. I would not have started a new publishing house in my mid-fifties if I was hopelessly downcast. But one must be realistic and realize that life for the purveyors of new and independent thought has become increasingly difficult. This is not to say that it has become impossible, but much more determination and imagination are needed to survive now than was the case in the past.

I can only speak for my own profession, but there we have seen exciting and innovative experiments. My publisher in Sweden, Ordfront, was created as a reader's cooperative with some thirty-thousand members. If only one-tenth of those buy a given book, the group's demanding titles can survive economically. Our author Pierre Bourdieu, who was France's leading sociologist, created in his Collège de France office a tiny firm that managed to show that all of France's established publishers had been wrong in saying that an audience for left-wing political criticism no longer existed. Some of his titles, admittedly including a few written by himself, sold in the hundreds of thousands of copies and forced the large firms to rethink their policies.

When The New Press was founded, I heard from my European colleagues that the folks at Random House were busily assuring them that our experiment would soon fail, that there was no sense entrusting manuscripts to us. Seventeen years later we are in the anomalous position of being able to publish dozens of titles each year that the large firms "can no longer afford to take on," as they explain to these same European colleagues and to their own authors.

But the fact that these small islands of independence still exist should not blind us to the seriousness of the overall situation. It is too easy to say, as many do, that the conglomerate control of nearly all of publishing is not so bad, since the small firms can still publish the poetry, the fiction, the translations, the cutting-edge political books that the larger publishers have abandoned. All of us together account for well under 1 percent of the books sold in any given year, and the hundred-plus university presses account for another 1 percent. Important as this 2 percent may be, it can not replace the huge flow of such books that used to come from nearly all of the major firms. In today's climate, it is hopeless to expect our government to use the antitrust laws that should have prevented these conglomerates from being created in the first place. But this does not mean that we should accept as inevitable the process that has dominated our intellectual life during the recent decades. There are still moral and practical decisions that can be taken to challenge these trends, by reviewers, by booksellers, and most importantly by authors. The decisions taken by Studs Terkel, in moving from Pantheon to the New Press, or by Kurt Vonnegut, in moving from Bertelsmann to the small independent Seven Stories Press, have made all the difference to their publishers' ability to survive.

I suppose it is my old reformer instincts that keep me from accepting the status quo as permanent in our lives. Reason would suggest that this is indeed what has happened. But in this case, I have to go against my Cartesian upbringing and hope that some form of resistance will continue, unlikely as its chances of ultimate success may be. Certainly I know from my own recent experience, and from that of my colleagues, that it is a far better and happier life outside the whale than inside.

After a dozen years at The New Press, feeling that we were safe for the immediate future and that my younger colleagues could get along very well without me on a daily basis, I made a totally unexpected decision: My wife Maria Elena and I decided to take a year away from New York and see what a different life might be like. Our initial decision to go back to Paris for a year in 2003 was not based on a dramatic need to go back to my roots or anything of the sort. I had been visiting Paris every year for more than forty years, stopping for a fortnight before going on to the annual Frankfurt Book Fair. I enjoyed these visits and felt that I knew Paris relatively well. I always felt like an American visitor, though a comfortable one.

My decision was based more on a simple feeling of fatigue with life in New York, a city that, after more than sixty years, I felt I knew too well. Our routine was too established, our life too predictable. Like many people my age, I felt a need to see if we could lead a different existence.

It was a small incident that led me to question the logic of my daily life. It started when my colleagues in the office next-door started sending me e-mails. I hated e-mails, and when I discovered that they were replacing the comfortable conversations that we used to have, I began to wonder why I was stubbornly staying in my New York office, nice as it was, when I could be someplace infinitely pleasanter. I asked Maria Elena what she thought of our spending the next year in Paris and found that she was even more enthusiastic than I. Having spent forty-two years in publishers' offices, I found that Manhattan life had lost some of its allure. Paris, at least, would be different.

There remained only the question of keeping in touch with our children. Natalia, our younger daughter, had lived in London with her British husband and her three children for many years. So, it would be far easier to see them all, with the train from Paris taking under three hours. Anya, our older daughter, lived just a few blocks from us on the Upper West Side, but she and her husband were such world travelers that we felt we would see them nearly as often. Both daughters, we hoped, would enjoy seeing our Paris life as much as we would.

What followed seemed incredibly easy. We discovered that Paris rental apartments are plentiful and inexpensive. Looking on the Web, we found that a furnished two-bedroom in central Paris could cost much less than our New York apartment. Through friends, we soon found something that sounded promising, even though we had only the vaguest idea of what it would actually look like. The only catch was permission to stay and work in Paris, but we were lucky in that respect. My wife is Spanish and therefore benefited from the EEC rules allowing her to live in Europe wherever she wanted. I was still considered a French citizen. When we had fled the German occupation in 1941 we did so with French passports, and in the French government's eyes once a Frenchman, always a Frenchman.

But the horrendous difficulties of leaving France when we did had left me with a deeply repressed distrust of French bureaucracy. I showed up at the consulate in New York fearing the worst and discovered quickly how much France had changed. To be sure, my old 1940s passport immediately drew a crowd of fascinated bureaucrats, who had never seen so ancient a document. Its handwritten pages were clearly antediluvian. My new documents spat out of the computer in just a few minutes, and within the hour I had my voter's card and identity card. Only my French medicare card was missing (which I would obtain in Paris with equal ease). The whole process had been infinitely easier than renewing my American passport.

Maria Elena and I decided then to write down a list of other fears we had about our move to Paris. On the whole, they proved equally baseless. We thought that everyday life in Paris would be needlessly complicated—difficult shopping, no deliveries, rude French people correcting our accents, the works. What we discovered from the very first day was that life was infinitely easier than it had been on the Upper West Side of New York. Within a block of our new apartment was everything we could possibly need. Three butchers, five bakery-patiserries, a fish shop and a tri-weekly market that made us swoon. There was a huge choice of fresh and tempting foods, much cheaper and more varied than New York. Our fish lady left the Normandy port of Honfleur at four o'clock every morning with that day's catch—fresher than anything we'd ever eaten. Should we ever get bored with the dozens of French market stands, there was a selection of Arab and Caribbean delicacies, and down the street were richer and more varied Italian and Greek delis than anything we'd ever encountered on Ninth Avenue in New York. The stallholders were admirably friendly, and many were of non-French origin—African, Arab, Vietnamese, Caribbean. And, with close to a half-million Chinese living in a series of Chinese-Vietnamese neighborhoods as extensive as any in Queens or Brooklyn, Paris had become nearly as multicultural as New York.

So, being a foreigner in Paris was hardly a novelty and being American brought no rebukes or unpleasant wisecracks. It was assumed that we were as opposed to Bush as the Parisians were. And as we read the very thorough coverage of the Iraq War, we couldn't help but feel that a steady diet of this kind of analysis would have converted even those Americans who had been persuaded to back Bush by the American media.

Reading *Le Monde*, and sometimes *Libération* and *Le Figaro*, every day was a revelation. Whatever their political affiliation, the papers were unanimous in their opposition to Bush's policies. But the reporting was thorough and intelligent, totally lacking the self-censorship and apologetics of their American counterparts. When I was giving a media course at the graduate school of Sciences-Po, the French equivalent of the London School of Economics, my students gasped in disbelief when they were assigned that day's copy of *USA Today* or the *Wall Street Journal* or even the *International Herald Tribune*. But when it came to French politics, the French press was far tamer—much slower to criticize the government, leaving uncovered vast problem areas of French politics and society. Areas that I assumed would be the focus of hot debate were barely discussed and seismic shifts in power were hardly protested. The more I followed the French media, the more I was struck by its silences and lacunae. The many corrupt dealings with Algeria and the former French colonies were hardly ever mentioned. Nor was the fate of the immigrants from those former colonies, who now were into their second and third generations in France, ever discussed. The press lacked reporters from those communities. The explosion of riots in Paris and other suburbs in 2005 should not have taken anyone by surprise. Nor should there have been such a lack of informed journalists to analyze those events. (*Le Monde* managed to bring in one reporter of North African origin from their Lyons bureau, and the others could do no better.)

This gradual discovery of French conformity was my biggest surprise—the last thing I expected in a country famous for its intellectual debates. During my annual publishing visits I had found hints of this, but I did not expect the general mood to be so quiescent. I knew there were a number of our major authors, such as Chomsky and Hobsbawm, for whom I could find no French publisher, in spite of their international renown. (Both would finally appear in French—but from small Belgian publishers!)

My French publisher asked if I'd write a sequel to *The Business of Books* on what I'd discovered during my year in Paris. When it was published, the reviews were friendly on the whole, but they failed to mention any of my criticisms of the French media, proving my point in a way I would have gladly avoided. To be sure, when *The Business of Books* came out in France some five years ago, the reviewers all agreed that I had painted a horrendous picture of what had happened in the U.S. and England, but that such conglomeration could never happen in France. Ironically, during the year I spent in Paris, the French media became much more concentrated than anything we'd seen in America or the rest of Europe (Berlusconi's Italy excepted).

* * *

But such weaknesses in the public sphere were not to be found in private. The people we met and worked with were welcoming and wonderfully friendly—they listened to my criticisms politely and sometimes, I think, in agreement. Talking is still one of the great French pastimes and in private one hears a great deal of criticism, particularly from people inside the media. But clearly the media's close links with the Chirac government had created a kind of corporatist coziness that is far more reminiscent of the corrupt French politics of the thirties than one would have expected it could be today.

I suspect that part of the problem is that, since daily life is so pleasant for most people, it's very easy to retreat into the pleasures of living in France and particularly of living in Paris. Most people have seven weeks' vacation in addition to working only a thirty-five-hour week, and this makes for a very relaxed pace— sometimes too relaxed for Americans as we discovered in August, when most of Paris closes down.

The French are understandably obsessed with the quality of their food, which contributes to this pleasant life. A Cornell professor of French history, Steven L. Kaplan, became a major celebrity by writing an incredibly detailed and very useful guide to Paris bread shops. (In our first year there, he told us that we lived between two of the best in Paris. The pleasure with which one could look forward to one's daily bread certainly added to the quality of life.)

As everyone who's ever been to Paris knows, just walking down the street is a source of endless surprise and pleasure. The variety of buildings, the wealth of gardens, and the warrens of lit-tle streets from another era all make the city an inexhaustible visu-al treat. The French know this and work at it. The city is impecca-bly clean. Each year thousands of new trees are planted and acres of new gardens are created. Where the Brits under Margaret Thatcher slashed away at streetcleaning along with every other public service, the French expanded theirs. (Not to mention that a ride on the Paris metro costs one-quarter as much as one on the London tube and the trains are far less crowded.) The city's charms are thus a result of careful social planning—not just the measures that preserve and renew architecture, but the constant care with which gardens are tended and green spaces extended. Living close to the Luxembourg gardens, we saw on a daily basis the amazing attention given to every tree and every planting. No gardening enthusiast ever spent as much time as the Paris park people do on their public spaces. No matter how small most Parisian apartments may be, the minute you step outside you are able to live as if you were in Versailles.

Not satisfied with the city's existing glories, Paris' Socialist mayor has embarked on a series of experiments designed to make the city an even more enjoyable place. I suspect there must be a deputy mayor in charge of Fun, whose only task is to open the city up for new pleasures. Much has been written about the summer beach on the Seine, where sand, beach chairs, and palm trees are installed in midsummer and which is visited by more than 3 mil-lion people each year. Visiting there myself, I was impressed by the degree to which people were simply enjoying themselves— whether having a nap on the specially built sleeping areas or join-ing in a sing-along of French popular music.

The idea that a city could successfully program these simple pleasures without any feeling of artificiality was impressive—priority was given to fun rather than to the demands of traffic flow or municipal dignity. Volleyball courts were established in front of the city hall, along with outdoor movie screens. The symbolism was clear and widely enjoyed. Less has been said about the decision to turn major arteries over to roller-bladers. Once a week one can see literally tens of thousands of youngsters zipping down the boulevards on a Friday evening. Once a year, the city's public buildings are illuminated and open all night for a *nuit blanche*, in which everyone is invited to spend the night visiting new places and ending up for free croissants and coffee in front of city hall. Far from being menacing, the streets at night are theirs to enjoy. These innovations cost very little, but they give the Parisians a unique feeling of ownership. Clearly these ideas could be replicated elsewhere, even if many of Paris' pleasures cannot.

But I must admit that writing this is a bit like describing New York by writing only about Central Park and not mentioning Harlem or the Bronx, because central Paris is increasingly a city of the rich. A recent census pointed out that one out of every eight Parisians lives well below the poverty line. Many of them live in the northern *arondissements*—the Eighteenth, Nineteenth, and Twentieth districts, which are inhabited in large part by immigrants and people of North African descent. But most of the poor live largely outside of Paris in the infamous *banlieus*—housing projects that surround the city much like those in American ghettos—which have become increasingly depressed and dangerous. Roughly 10 percent of the French are now of Arab origin, and France's failure to integrate this population is its major crisis. An occasional minister talks of confronting the 50 percent unemployment rate among the young, but the problem needs far greater resources than the present Conservative government is willing to devote, not that the Socialists have done much better. The result is that the French have chosen to address the symptoms, as in the law forbidding veils in public schools, rather than the underlying causes. The explosion of the Paris suburbs in 2005 grew out of this neglect. And the situation was only exacerbated when the ambitious and demagogic interior minister, Nicaolas Sarkozy, decided to compete with ultra-right-wing leader Jean-Marie Le Pen in playing the anti-immigrant card. Under Sarkozy's orders, the local police changed from a relatively benign policy of neighborhood policing to one of aggressively checking young people for ID papers, which created endless tensions and feelings of humiliation among the immigrant population. All this became a tinderbox waiting to explode.

This has also fueled the antagonism and fighting between young Arab kids and their Jewish counterparts in the country's schools—which in turn have given rise to reports of French anti-Semitism. It is certainly true that the government, fearful of antagonizing its Islamic minority, was terribly slow in cracking down on these schoolyard assaults, but from what I could see, the problem was not in French anti-Jewish feeling per se. None of the documentary films and articles that I saw, some of them by the most militant of Jewish authors, came up with any evidence of a general problem—beyond Le Pen's ludicrous and self-destructive comments in defense of the German occupation and of the Gestapo (as if he was deliberately seeking to destroy his National Front party before being forced to retire). Indeed, the official stance has been remarkably firm. Unlike François Mitterrand's ambiguous pro-Vichy origins, Jacques Chirac has gone out of his way to condemn past anti-Semitic behavior. His government declared a national day of mourning on the anniversary of the notorious Vel 'd'Hiv roundup of French Jews (when the French police arrested many of the 75,000 Jews who were later killed).

All this has come late. Many Paris schools now bear a plaque in memory of the 11,000 French schoolchildren deported and killed by the Germans with the full cooperation of Vichy. But this homage was due to the efforts of Serge Klarsfeld, the famous Nazi-hunter, and the plaques were affixed only in January of 2003.

The little street where we lived much of our first year was hardly a typical one. Only one block long, it runs from the popular Place de la Contre-Escarpe to the Rue Monge, near the Panthéon. At the top of the street, a plaque marks the house where Hemingway lived during the twenties. Right next to it is the building where Descartes dwelled. A little further down, opposite our own door, is yet another plaque, marking the place where the philosopher Benjamin Fondane had lived, simply giving his date of birth and the place of his death: Auschwitz. Fondane had been a friend of my father's in the thirties, one of the many whose death he learned of when we were safely in New York.

It was dealing with the past that turned out to be the most difficult part of that first year in Paris. America is, more than ever, a country of immigrants, and part of this tradition is that no one asks where you came from or who you were. For more than sixty years in New York, I rarely spoke of my parents. Very few people, outside of my children, cared. As is obvious from these pages, their life was completely different from mine. Alas, my father died before I had a chance to find out more about his past, an-all-too common complaint among people my age. But in putting together his correspondence I began to learn much of what has led to my writing this book.

In Paris, being my father's son turned out to be a full-time job. For those in the world of letters, he was still very much a living presence. The books he had created, the Pléiade series of French classics, were at the front of every serious bookstore and in every home that had any books at all. Graduate students asked to look through his papers for their thesis work. Every press interview started with the fact that I was his son. When we published the collection of his correspondence with Gide, the press covered it extensively, well aware of the role he had played in French intellectual life and the way in which his role had been terminated.

I only wish that my mother could have seen all this. Her own brief return to France after my father's death had been a great disappointment to her. At my urging, she had gone back to visit Paris while I was in college. But the links to her family had been strained by the war's separation and this must have affected the way she felt about returning. She came back to New York complaining about the way the city had changed. The Champs-Élysées was now filled with ads and neon, she lamented, and was no longer the pure and dignified avenue she remembered. I assume that beneath these, no doubt, real disappointments was the greater sadness of feeling that she could no longer go back, that her life there could not be restarted, that New York, for all of its faults, had become her home. She lived only a few years longer— long enough, luckily, to see the birth of our two daughters. But she would never share my own trips back or the pleasure with which I would gradually rediscover France.

My annual visits had been a mixed blessing. I had greatly enjoyed them and gradually began to feel that I could participate in French life, could meet and indeed publish many of those whose work I admired. But there was always a feeling of being rushed; there was never enough time to do all that I wanted to do, to see more of the city than the familiar streets around the publishing houses in Saint Germain, to meet family and friends as well as publishing colleagues.

My first year in Paris led me to feel that all this could be repaired, that I could now take the time to see the city thoroughly, to do the exploring, both physical and intellectual, that I had only just begun. Maria Elena and I decided that we would find an apartment in which we could, in the future, live half of each year, and much of that year was spent looking for the ideal place. It turned out to be the perfect way to explore the city. We went to practically every neighborhood, looked at more than a hundred apartments, and finally settled on the place in which we have lived since, every spring and summer. Although we each had our own list of sometimes contradictory criteria, the apartment we found—in a small 1925 building in the Marais—came as close as was possible to satisfying us both.

With the dreaded Internet, I found I could easily continue my editorial work and even keep up with the American media. Life, it turned out, could be bifurcated in this way. In the fall and winter, we could enjoy our New York routine and see our old friends, and I could work directly with my authors. But the rest of the year would be French for the both of us. It was a somewhat schizophrenic existence, but one that mirrored the inner divide that I had spent so many years pretending not to notice.

I am still very much an American in Paris, obsessed with what is happening in the United States, doing what I can to try to change our disastrous policies. In France, I can afford the luxury of still being a foreigner, not having to involve myself in all the local battles that need to be fought. Yet I follow these closely, too; I talk about them endlessly with our French friends and feel very close to the issues, past and present, that still divide this country. I can also luxuriate in the feeling that most of the French still share the politics that I have clung to over the years. A recent poll showed that two-thirds of the population did not feel that the free market was the way the country should go in the future (as opposed to the opposite percentages in Britain). The French still look to the state to collectively solve many of their problems. They do not accept that profitable factories should be shut down to improve a conglomerate's balance sheets. The inevitability of globalized capitalism is not accepted. Indeed, the French have invented the term *capitalisme sauvage*—a wild, untamed capitalism, ravenous and dangerous.

In spite of the many political views that I share with the French, there are still vast cultural and social differences that I cannot overcome. I can never make up for the years when I didn't live there, for the French education I never had, for all the books that are part of everyone's background in this country that I never read. But I can gradually rediscover some of what I have missed, read the Pléiade volumes that I grew up with but rarely had time for, begin to recapture the history and culture of the years that my parents so enjoyed while they were here. Simple pleasures, but a happy ending to this story.